Nashville's

Mother Church:

The History of the

Ryman Auditorium

D1214271

William U. Eiland

Nashville's Mother Church: The History of the Ryman Auditorium
©1992 Opryland USA Inc.
All rights reserved.

Library of Congress Catalog Card Number: 92-71670

ISBN 0-9633010-0-4

Text by William U. Eiland
Printed by Thomas-Parris Printing, Old Hickory, Tennessee
Designed and edited by Trish McGee
Front and back cover design by David Paine
Cover photograph hand-tinted by Meryl Truett

Acknowledgments

The author wishes to acknowledge gratefully the assistance of the following individuals and institutions:

Hal Durham; Steve Buchanan; Rachel Sanders; Bob Kimbro; Mary Lou Gallagher; Mrs. Virginia Lyle and her coworkers at the Metropolitan Nashville-Davidson County Archives; Vanderbilt University Library Special Collections; the Nashville Room, Nashville-Davidson County Public Library; Tennessee State Library and Archives; Hargrett Rare Book and Manuscript Library, University of Georgia Libraries; Special Collections, Robert W. Woodruff Library, Emory University; the Country Music Foundation Library; the Tennessee Performing Arts Center; *Roselawn,* the home of Sam P. Jones in Cartersville, Ga.; Louise Davis; Glen Thompson; Judy Mizell; Ronnie Pugh; John Rumble; Sarah Harwell; Jody Lentz; Tom Camden; and Mrs. Lucy C. Mulcahy, grandniece of Sam P. Jones, who proved by her wealth of knowledge and the kindness of her hospitality that being the beneficiary of the graciousness of a southern lady is reward in itself for asking questions. Mr. Roy A. Miles, Jr., the last recording secretary for the Auditorium Improvement Company, kindly allowed me the use of unpublished corporate documents and letters in his possession, and to him I owe particular indebtedness for his time and advice.

I also must thank those entertainers who showed by their friendliness, their candor, and their willingness to help that the notion of the Grand Ole Opry as family is no fiction. Thomas B. Brumbaugh, Andrew Ladis, and Evelyn Wiley read the manuscript and gave helpful suggestions for its improvement.

To all of them, I offer sincere thanks.

Contents

Introduction

Some may find the Ryman Auditorium an unlikely shrine. Lacking in architectural distinction, surrounded by a section of Nashville many of its residents would rather ignore, and cited often in its history as a safety hazard, the old building endures. Like a magnet whose attraction is almost irresistible, the Ryman continues to draw thousands of visitors to Nashville every year. While it is true that tourists come for many reasons, true country music fans make it a special point to visit the "Old Opry House," "The Ryman," or "The Mother Church," as it is variously known.

For a little while those visitors can experience some of the magic which persists in the worn, wooden interior. They can stand on the stage where Patsy Cline poured out her heartfelt longings, where Roy Acuff let loose his "Wabash Cannonball," and where Uncle Dave Macon handled his banjo "like a monkey handles a peanut."

Many will remember hot summer nights when the music, loud and sweet, spoke directly to their hearts, when "corny" jokes were somehow funnier and more innocent when shared by strangers drawn together by their love of country music and its stars. They will recall hand fans beating the heavy air, splinters sticking in the seats of their pants, and popcorn kernels crunching underfoot.

When asked, most can tell you exactly what spot on which pew they sat on their first visit—who sang, who danced and who told jokes. Some may even tell you exactly what they were wearing that night. A lady interviewed on one of her annual pilgrimages to Hank Williams' gravesite recalled: "My momma bought me a new, blue dress that was made out of some of that frilly stuff in the skirt for my first trip to the Opry. Well, when I heard ole Hank, I kept jumpin' up and down, and those dang pews tore my pretty dress to shreds in the back. But, I didn't care. I wouldn't take anything for that old tattered thing, 'cause that's what I wore when I first heard Hank. Still got it and show it to my grandchildren."

Nashville's society matrons may have less happy memories of the Ryman's hard benches, for they too sat there through performances by the great opera stars and by the legends of the American theater. Throughout its history, the Ryman has been a community institution where political debates, graduations, talent shows, and club meetings vied for space on its busy schedule.

Before Hank Williams ever hunched over the microphone stage center, Enrico Caruso threw back his head and golden, perfect notes soared heavenward. Before Dolly Parton and Porter Wagoner sang their duets in the Ryman, Nelson Eddy and Jeanette MacDonald warbled their love calls. Before Minnie Pearl's "Howdee!" raised the rafters, Billy Sunday's "Repent!" thundered back in echoes.

Nashville's Ryman is indeed a special place. It is the same age as New York's Carnegie Hall, and it is arguable which has the more distinguished history. One thing is certain: no other tabernacle has been so catholic. What other auditorium can boast a revival, *Hamlet*, a prize fight, an ice show, and the Grand Ole Opry all on the same stage? What other building can lay claim to Dwight L. Moody, Booker T. Washington, Sarah Bernhardt, Hawkshaw Hawkins, and Trigger among the ghosts who haunt its walls.

Truly as many stories abound about the Ryman as there are bricks in its walls. Indeed, the history of the Ryman Auditorium is the history of Nashville in the twentieth century. Yet, it is more: a history of popular culture and entertainment in the United States from the Gilded Age to the Nixon Era. It is a story which can be divided with deceptive convenience into its pre-Opry years and post-Opry years, but, like all such easy classifications, the reality is much more complex, much richer in detail, and much more fascinating than such division allows.

The history of a place is given meaning by those who,

2

however briefly, inhabited it. Rednecks and bluebloods, tragedians and clowns, saints and sinners: they all spent time there. But of this motley crowd three remarkable people occupy center stage in the non-Opry history of the old red brick building in downtown Nashville: Sam Jones, Captain Tom Ryman, and Lula Naff all contributed to the legend that is the Ryman Auditorium, a legend given international voice through WSM Radio and the Grand Ole Opry.

Happily, the Ryman's story is incomplete. For the first word in that history we have Sam Jones' denunciations of sin in Nashville. We do not yet have and hope there will not be a final word.

Samuel P. Jones
Hargrett Rare Book and Manuscript Library, University of Georgia, Athens

I. Prologue: The Tabernacle

At the end of the nineteenth century, Nashville's uncontested preeminence as a cultural, educational, and commercial center for the post-Reconstruction South was a source of great pride to its citizenry. Rapidly modernizing, the city became one of the most important rail centers in the region, having already established itself as a prominent riverport. Adding to the hustle and bustle of steamboat and railroad, the first electric streetcars began service in the late 1880s over the newly paved streets. Nashville was busily distancing herself from the bitterness of the Civil War and joining the ranks of the industrializing cities of America in the Gay '90s.

To contemporary observers, Nashville's position was evident. It was the main commercial center and market for the entire region; it was a burgeoning financial center; and its publishing and educational establishments gave it prestige throughout the nation. It was then for good reasons that Nashvillians took pleasure in calling their city the "Athens of the South."

In 1892 her population stood at 77,000 people. Only twelve years earlier the U.S. Bureau of the Census had given the population as 43,350. This unprecedented growth in part accounted for the development of what has been called Nashville's "Decisive Decade," the years between 1890 and 1900, precisely those years when the Union Gospel Tabernacle became a forum for religious revival, public discussion, and cultural and educational entertainment.

While urban expansion and increasing industrialization were noteworthy results of its population explosion, so were social

5

unrest and severe overcrowding. As the "haves" prospered, the "have nots" became more apparent, and Nashvillians became alarmed at such manifestations of social unrest as rising crime, public drunkenness, and pervasive poverty. Lower Broadway with its saloons, gambling, and prostitution was an affront to those moralists who were being swept along by the strong current of revivalism engulfing the nation.

Revivalism was one response to the social ills and the loosening of those Victorian inhibitions which had heretofore governed behavior, and with the coming of the professional revivalist to town, Nashville's religious and cultural life would never be the same.

The rise of the modern city provided a fertile environment for the professional evangelist. So much sin in such a compact space not only attracted the sinner but the self-styled saint as well. Dwight L. Moody's evangelistic success showed others just how popular, and how profitable, revivalism could be. When local churches proved unable or unwilling to stem the tide of lawlessness and iniquity, the city evangelist stepped in, and by shrewd self-promotion of his message to an event-starved populace, he was often able to effect changes by the sheer force of a powerful personality. Most important, these revival preachers reached many people who had lost contact for one reason or another with local religious institutions.

Enormously influential in the South, Samuel Porter Jones was just such a man. His impact on Nashville was immediate. Unprepared for his flamboyance, the city did not quite know how to react when he first came to town in March 1885. Nonetheless, what began as a two-day revival sponsored by and within local churches became a longer-lasting spirit of Christian, primarily Protestant, renewal that had far greater results than the Reverend Jones himself would ever have imagined.

If heredity does in fact have the power to shape us, it is hardly surprising that Sam Jones became the leading evangelist of his day. Although his grandfather, great-grandfather, and four uncles were Methodist ministers, it must have been from his grandmother that he got his zeal and determination. It is said that she read the Bible thirty-seven times, each time on her knees, and demonstrated her faith in the otherwise staid hometown church by clapping loudly, shouting lustily, and walking the aisles whenever she felt the presence of the Holy Spirit. She took care of young Sam when, as he described himself, he was a "black eyed, mischievous, frolicksome lad . . . so smart that the teachers were compelled to like him, so bad that he acquired a close and practical intimacy with the rod."

Though he imagined himself cut out for greatness even as a child, Jones spent five years of his early life in drunken dissipation. In 1872, at his father's deathbed, he promised to "meet his father in heaven," as penance for having sent the old soldier "in sorrow to his grave." True to his word, he became an itinerant preacher that same year, and his experiences among the rural folk of his north Georgia circuit accounted for his intensely personal and deliberately homespun style of preaching. His pattern of first raking his audiences over the hot coals of hell and then salving their burning wounds with the promise of sweet redemption gained for him a reputation as a fiery, charismatic speaker. By 1883 his fame had spread to the point that he could devote himself to full-time revivalism, and this he did with a vengeance.

Such a man invading a town that prided itself on being a religious center was bound to arouse controversy. His habit of plain speaking provoked accusations from the religious establishment and the press that he was vulgar, coarse, even obscene. A man who matter of factly said that he was proud to call "a spade a spade and a hog a hog," and mean by that one of Nashville's leading citizens, aroused ire and indignation among his more self-satisfied listeners.

In those March revivals of 1885 Jones castigated Nashvillians for their indifference to sin. He painted the city as top to bottom a den of the worst kind of depravity, with the most visible signs of that immorality whiskey drinking, card playing, dancing, and clubbing—precisely those diversions his listeners at McKendree Methodist Church were most likely to pursue.

Their social clubs he called "gilded deviltry." Dancing was for simpletons, and Jones begged mothers not to debauch their daughters by sending them to "dancing-schools kept by old hook-nosed Frenchmen." The Reverend Jones told Nashville that he had nothing but pity for the poor man to whom the devil donated a society woman and a poodle dog. Other targets for his contempt were gambling, prostitution, circuses, profanity, billiards, dresses "cut down low," baseball ("the most corrupting thing this side of hell"), bicycle riding, prize fighting, and cigarettes ("an effeminate Yankee convention which softens the brain").

Of all human sins whiskey drinking was the worst. For Jones, as he shouted to his audience in Nashville, "every barroom is a recruiting office for hell." Whiskey may be a good thing in its place, "but its place was in hell!" How, he asked, could any city which licensed eighty-one wholesale liquor dealers and ninety saloons ever raise itself from its quagmire of degradation?

Lashing out at laxity and selfishness, Jones proclaimed himself as a scourge to the good, but not quite good enough, people of Nashville. Louise Proctor Ryman remembered from her elders what "Sam Jones colorfully said after the congregation had just finished singing 'In the Sweet Bye and Bye.' He stood up to preach and announced that his subject was not on 'The Sweet Bye and Bye,' but rather on the 'The Filthy Here and Now.'"

For the next two months Sam Jones, the man, and his message were the talk of Nashville. While many thought he had delivered a timely and necessary inspiration to Nashville's Christian brethren, others thought colorful language and pulpit histrionics decidedly out of place in their city. It had been particularly galling to some to hear Jones advise Nashville's mothers to marry their daughters to mulattoes rather than to card players or to drunkards.

Jones himself added fuel to the fire by calling his critics at Nashville's various newspapers "sap-headed reporters." He sometimes came dangerously close to comparing his enemies to dogs but stopped short, as he put it, because he "wouldn't want to hurt the dog's feelings." No wonder some Nashvillians hoped the Lord would spare them the return of Mr. Jones and his acid tongue.

But return he did in May 1885 for a series of revivals which Nashville's *Daily American* reported "brought together the largest congregation ever gathered in the South." True to form, Jones never tempered his remarks. Exhorting the people of Nashville to wash off the "devil's fleas," he accused them of every sin imaginable, including some not previously hurled their way—adultery, hypocrisy, and usury.

In spite of critics, Jones' popularity proved so great that plans immediately got under way to provide him with a permanent meeting place for his revivals. He represented a new force in Nashville, and the city's leaders were anxious to use this new social Christianity's emphasis on good works, rather than on grace, for their own ends. Sam Jones' "git up and git" brand of religion was a revelation for a city long viewed as a citadel of traditional Protestantism. The lasting symbol of this muscular Christianity of organized philanthropy and legal temperance reform is the Ryman Auditorium.

Thomas Green Ryman
Tennessee State Library and Archives

Captain Thomas Green Ryman

Twenty-three years after the arrival of the first steamboat on the Cumberland River, Thomas Green Ryman was born in south Nashville on October 12, 1841. At an early age, when his family moved to Chattanooga, young Tom learned about the ways of river life by fishing with his father in the Tennessee River. That experience quickly proved valuable. By 1860 the family had returned to Nashville, and with the death of his father shortly thereafter, Tom became the sole support of his mother, brother, and three sisters.

Ryman's fishing business thrived during the Civil War. He sold his catch to both Union and Confederate forces and thereby saved enough money to purchase his first steamboat. To buy it, he had to go to New Orleans, an arduous journey in those days. Having sewn $3,500 into his shirt, he refused to take it off even at night. Later he would say that along the hot, muggy trails to Louisiana, he "like to have smothered to death" before he could buy the boat.

Ryman's first steamboat had the appropriate name *Alpha*, and it quickly made enough money to enable him to build his second steamer, the *Eddyville*, in 1869. By 1880 he had two packet companies operating on the Cumberland and lower Ohio Rivers, and in 1885 he consolidated these into the Ryman Line with a total fleet of some thirty-five steamers.

Although barely literate, Ryman was industrious and shrewd. He had to be both to withstand the sometimes underhanded tactics to which his competitors on the river resorted.

Physically strong and well-proportioned, he was a tough man who could easily handle the rough and hard-living stevedores he employed.

By some accounts he was also a soft-hearted man who distributed coal to the needy from his own basement, who paid for the funerals of his employees and saw to it that their families did not suffer, and who even had his gardener go out and rake the snow from a magnolia's leaves lest the tree be too much "offended" at the weight.

At times it is difficult to separate the myth of Captain Ryman from his reality. Some versions of his life hold that he was an "extraordinary reprobate," much given to carousing with his rowdies before his conversion. Certain it is that Ryman owned a saloon on Broad Street where roustabout and passenger jostled each other to buy cheap whiskey at a nickel a glass. It is not hard to believe the legend that he went with some of his unruly cronies to Brother Jones' revival tent for the express purpose of disrupting the meeting with heckling and jeering.

But mysterious indeed are the ways of the Lord, and at Sam Jones' first meeting of May 10, 1885, Captain Ryman converted to a Christianity of good works, civic virtue, and gospel evangelism. Many writers have said that he became a changed man after hearing Jones speak of the sanctity of motherhood. A complete version of Jones' first sermon in May does not exist, but it is safe to assume that he painted vivid pictures of a mother's tribulations when her son turns to drink, because elsewhere he brought tears to the eyes of his congregations when he described the good mother grieving over her son's descent into a drunkard's hell.

Again legend takes over where facts are few. Local historians have said that Ryman immediately rounded up his friends, went to his saloon, gathered the whiskey barrels, and poured their contents into the Cumberland. Remarking that "they say even the fish got tipsy," one Nashvillian gave new expression to the tale that Ryman was so beset by remorse over the whiskey trade on his steamboats that he began telegraphing up and down the rivers to his boat captains that they should break up the bars and dump the liquor and gambling tables overboard.

Far more likely, he simply let the contracts for bar services expire and did not renew them. His daughter Daisy Ryman Coggins confirmed that the liquor on board his boats was not his property but that of the concessionnaires who had contracted with the company to run the bars. Regardless, it was a costly decision for Ryman since he lost both his percentage of the bar profits and those customers who would have preferred more rapid rail transport were it not for the liveliness of his shipboard bars and gaming parlors.

On the night of his conversion Ryman discussed with Jones the idea of building a "Tabernacle for all denominations that would be amply large to accommodate the largest crowd," but appeals for the Young Men's Christian Association building, which were then in progress (and for which Sam Jones would raise much of the money from his congregations) took precedence, and they decided to postpone their plans.

In the meantime, since he had to delay his more grandiose vision, Ryman built a gospel and temperance hall at 57 Broad Street. As he reported in a letter of March 17, 1886, to Reverend Jones, he built the hall for $3,500 with the assistance of another convert and associate, Captain Alex Kendall. The Captains' temperance hall was "run non sectarian," seated 250 people, and was open every night for an hour.

Captain Ryman also mounted "scripture boards" on street corners and outfitted a gospel wagon to serve as a sort of mobile mission in the city. Its headquarters was the temperance hall, conveniently located next to Ryman's offices. He then had scriptural passages painted over the doorways on his steamers lest passengers ever forgot that they rode on a vessel devoted to God's glory. Indeed, Sam Jones had no more zealous convert. Ryman revealed to the *Louisville Courier-Journal* that he "believes in the will of Divine Providence and never insures his boats."

Tom Ryman envisioned a grander, more appropriate building for evangelism than his small temperance hall. His opinion finally prevailed over those who were in favor of buying the old Broad Street Amusement Hall for Jones' revivals. Plans to build a suitable hall began when a Charter of Incorporation for the Union Gospel Tabernacle was filed on February 25, 1889. As expressly stated in its Articles, its goals were "strictly religious, non-sectarian, and non-denominational and for the purpose of promoting religion, morality and the elevation of humanity to a higher plane and more usefulness."

Ryman and the trustees of the new corporation quickly set

out to find a suitable location. In an interview in 1897 he recalled that "after days of hunting among real estate men, we bought the lot on which the Tabernacle stands." Although it had to be centrally located and convenient to public transportation, it could not have "street cars passing the building to annoy the meeting."

The trustees wasted no time in beginning construction, setting the foundations in the summer of 1889 and raising the walls to a height of six feet by spring of the following year. For the next several years Captain Ryman, Sam Jones, and the trustees sought funds to finish the building. Even when it was substantially complete, the new Tabernacle carried large debts for its construction, debts for which Captain Ryman continued to pay interest until his death.

Yet for Captain Ryman the building was worth its heavy cost. Even today this relic of the late Victorian age, beloved by those who experience its warm intimacy, never fails to impress the visitor. But how grand it must have seemed in the 1890s with its vast roof and the curving spaces of its interior. The building is imposing in its solidity, its unadorned strength, as if earnestness of purpose had been poured into its every brick. Ryman and his fellow trustees hoped to build the largest revival hall in the country, and even today, surrounded as it is by a motley collection of the old and new in architectural styles, it stands alone in gaunt splendor.

Ryman said that in 1887 he himself drew the first pencil sketch for the Tabernacle. Because of other things he said, we know that he dreamed of a building large enough to seat "multitudes." Ryman chose Hugh C. Thompson as the architect and J. G. Jones to build the foundation. According to a contemporary newspaper account, Thompson agreed to reduce his rates in order to have the honor of building the Tabernacle.

Though some critics have characterized the structure as graceless, Thompson eventually won admiration from his contemporaries and from modern builders for raising such a broad roof 100 feet from the ground at its peak.

The first revival held within the walls of the building occurred in May 1890. Ryman and his architect raised a tent over the walls and foundations, but in the face of thousands hungry to hear Sam Jones this was merely a stopgap measure. Both men knew that the building had to be finished before

14

another series of revivals could take place there.

The two years between 1890 and 1892 saw most of the final construction of the Tabernacle. Finding funds was always a problem, and for Captain Ryman, whose overriding passion had become that building, the construction meant a great deal of personal effort, most of it, as he put it, "on the streets." Before his death he said of his persistent search for money: "I have prayed to God when most people were asleep. I have worked for this Tabernacle hard for 10 years. I have neglected my business and paid out money liberally for it. So much have I done this that many people thought I had plenty of money. This is a mistake; I had my heart in it though."

True to the purposes stated in its Charter, the Tabernacle served as a center for religious revivalism in late nineteenth-century Nashville. In 1893 the trustees invited the famed Reverend T. DeWitt Talmadge to speak in Nashville at a one-night service. So popular was the event that hundreds were turned away at the door. Soon thereafter, the trustees planned another revival, this time featuring the Reverend B. Fay Mills, a celebrated professional evangelist whose "system" quickly gained converts wherever he preached.

Mills required a great deal of preliminary work by the local churches before his appearance, including arranging meetings for men only, for ladies only, and for young people only in the various churches. Nearly all of Nashville's Protestant churches planned to participate in this crusade. Advance organization paid dividends in souls, and, if anything, Mills' revival was more successful in fulfilling the goals of the Tabernacle and in unifying Nashville's Christians than even Jones had been, so much so that one of the local newspapers called it "the greatest awakening" in the city's history.

Sam Jones, of course, made annual visits to raise money for the Tabernacle, but the religious event of the year 1896 was Dwight L. Moody's two-week revival. Four thousand people had gathered in November the year before just to make preparations, and committees and subcommittees of laymen and clergy spent the intervening three months working out the details.

When the time came, Moody moved the city to a new height of spiritual fervor with his spare, gentle eloquence. He was tireless in speaking two or three times a day and to a variety of congregations throughout the city. Such was his influence and

15

popularity that the *Daily American* grandiosely proclaimed Nashville the center of the nation, a claim the editors would repeat for several years to come.

As if to prove the assertion, Sam Jones, the "Moody of the South," came again to Nashville a year later. He arrived with a purpose or, rather, had purpose thrust upon him. Many groups intended to hold conventions in Nashville that year to coincide with the Tennessee Centennial Exposition. One such group, the Confederate Veterans Association, promised to bring the largest convention ever held in Nashville to the Tabernacle if it could provide enough space for their meetings. Sam Jones set about to raise the money to build a gallery to provide that space.

The Captain still had Hugh Thompson's original plans for the Gallery, and mindful of the need to save money he and his committee accepted a low bid of around $10,000 for the iron and steel support construction, the woodwork, and enough seating for 2,500 people. The Louisville Bridge Company did the iron work, anchoring the Gallery on steel columns extending to the basement, and the Indiana Church Furnishing Company won the contract for the benches with a bid of $2,700. Those pews are the very ones still in the Auditorium, though some, unmarred by souvenir hunters hungry for the rosette decorations at the top, are preserved at Opryland.

J. H. Yeaman did the woodwork for the Gallery, and aside from minor work he and his fellow contractors finished the new gallery by the end of May. Since they needed hard cash and not pledges for much of their work, Ryman called on Sam Jones for an impromptu benefit for both the Gallery and the reunion funds, the latter's surplus eventually being applied to the former's debt.

On June 22, 1897, the reunion of Confederate Veterans— "the remnant of an army that is rapidly passing away . . . , gray with age and scarred with noble wounds," in the words of Governor Robert Taylor—brought nearly 100,000 people into Nashville, practically doubling the population of the city for three days. Nashville, proud of its progress and delighted to be hosting the Centennial Exposition, responded with a warm hospitality that had its citizens opening homes and schools to the veterans. The Tabernacle served as the group's headquarters and the starting point for a stirring parade through the streets of Nashville. Because of the nostalgia which they generated and

A view of the Confederate Gallery packed with people attending a revival. Note the Gothic window arches and the steel columns. Special Collections/Vanderbilt University Library

their contributions to the completion of the Tabernacle, the Veterans of 1897 left behind a lasting legacy when the trustees honored their convention by naming the new addition "The Confederate Gallery."

In 1897, then, Hugh Thompson's plans for the Union Gospel Tabernacle had been realized. Except for the building of the stage, the hall looked substantially as it does today, with its gabled, red brick facade set onto a rusticated stone base. Although it lacks the exuberance of late Victorian architecture, its impressive proportions and sturdy pier buttressing are Gothic in inspiration, as are its details: rows of lancet windows, the arcading of the roof parapets, and the pointed arch which enframes a dedicatory plaque on the facade. And additional decoration once relieved the spare austerity one sees today. Originally, the building had crest-tiles, that is, a row of stylized flowers such as in England's Exeter Cathedral, along the main roof line and ornamental crockets on the gables. The most spectacular achievement of its architect is the broad roof, which encloses such a vast space. In spite of its stained glass windows, it is best described architecturally as an auditorium, for it was

An early photograph of the Ryman shows the decoration along the roofline and the facade. Nashville Room/Nashville-Davidson County Public Library

built as one, and not as a church, though it may claim to be. Perhaps its ecclesiastical character is most evident in the rounded interior where the original wooden floors and pews are bathed in the warm lights from those colored windows, a later addition meant to reinforce the similarities to a church. In May 1899 the completed Tabernacle finally conformed to the intentions of Captain Ryman, Sam Jones, and Hugh Thompson. It seated 3,755 people and had cost approximately $100,000 to build.

The Tabernacle's directors could not easily ignore the public's participation in its construction. Many of them, Tom Ryman included, eventually realized that the Tabernacle belonged not to its trustees but to the people of Nashville, who were demanding that it be used for a variety of purposes. Tom Ryman, however, never lost his conviction that it should not be used for anything morally repugnant or frivolous. As time passed, and particularly after his death, the trustees leased the building for almost any program which they found suitable and which required a grander space than other buildings in Nashville

In 1892 the Theodore Thomas Orchestra gave the first concert in the Ryman. Tennessee State Library and Archives

could provide. They also realized early on that they would have to depend on non-religious events to bring in much-needed revenue to service the debt.

The first strictly secular event in the Tabernacle was probably Professor E. Warren Clark's illustrated lecture on Ponce de Leon, held on May 12–13, 1892. If not the first, at least the largest early performance in the nearly finished Tabernacle was by the Theodore Thomas Orchestra. Mr. Thomas was the well-known founder and conductor of the Chicago Symphony Orchestra, and the trustees unwisely hoped that paid admissions to a concert by his orchestra and chorus would pay the cost of his contract to appear. Other programs, particularly by his chorus, were necessary to pay those expenses, and the debt to him was finally canceled. His appearance unfortunately had added nothing to the sadly depleted building fund.

For the first twenty years of its existence, the Board of Directors relied on the Lyceums and Chatauquas to provide the entertainment demanded by the public. These were groups which supplied speakers and musicians to localities that would otherwise not have them. Through the services of these organizations, Commodore Matthew Perry, William Jennings Bryan,

John Philip Sousa and his Band, Thomas Dixon, and Alf and Robert Taylor appeared in the Auditorium. Of course, the community also used the building for a variety of purposes throughout its history. Meharry Medical School had its commencement activities there for many years. The Fisk University Jubilee Singers gave many concerts on its stage, and local high schools used it for their graduation ceremonies until late in its history.

Ward-Belmont College and Vanderbilt University sponsored musical series in the Ryman, and for a while it served as home to the Nashville Symphony Orchestra and to the Opera Guild. Policemen's associations, the American Red Cross, the ASPCA, and numerous ladies' clubs and churches, among others, used the building for fund-raising programs.

Churches in particular rented the Ryman for large gatherings. For example, the General Conference of the Colored Methodist Episcopal Church invited the great educator Booker T. Washington to address its convention in the Tabernacle in 1902. Revivals remained an integral part of the Ryman story throughout its history. N. B. Hardeman, Aimee Semple McPherson, Walt Holcomb, Gipsy Smith, and Norman Vincent Peale all conducted crusades from the building and drew crowds to hear their inspirational oratory.

None was more famous or gifted a preacher than Billy Sunday, who led revival meetings in the Auditorium in the twenties and thirties. Once, as Jack Norman, Sr. relates, the Reverend Sunday held a service at which he condemned lower Broadway and the red light district of Nashville as "the devil's backbone." He excoriated the city's fathers for allowing such goings-on in a so-called Christian city. On this occasion the crowd included two ladies who happened to be employed in that district and had come to hear the famous Reverend Sunday, probably more out of an unwholesome curiosity than geniune interest in salvation. Their curiosity satisfied, they did not remain to be saved. Mr. Norman finishes the story: "They arose and started to walk out. When Sunday saw this he could not resist the chance to further condemn, and shouted to the audience, 'See, there goes two daughters of the devil.'"

"Having nearly reached the exit, one of them turned, waved to Sunday and shouted back, 'Good-bye, Daddy!'"

Taking their cue from the preachers, politicians also found

the Auditorium an appropriate place for large meetings. In fact, the earliest controversy about the Tabernacle centered on its use during an election. And, despite its exalted credo, the Tabernacle came perilously close to charges of misuse when, in the fall of 1894, it was used for "strictly" political purposes, the Tennessee gubernatorial election conventions. Both Republicans and Democrats held speaking engagements and rallies there, but shortly Nashvillians noted that many of the building's backers were staunch Republicans who supported the party's nominee, H. Clay Evans. The Nashville papers, especially the *Daily American*, lampooned this group as advocates of a third political party, Tabernacleism, with Ryman and his "gang of pseudo-reformers" supporting the "Tabernacle Ticket." When Ryman carelessly stated that he was sure that the Tabernacle Ticket would win, Joseph W. Dillin, from the pulpit of the Auditorium itself, called Ryman's "gang" a "rag-tag, bob-tail, whop-it-up-together-and-throw-it-in-a-bag-ticket."

The political furor aroused by Tabernacleism humiliated Tom Ryman, and he wrote a letter to *The American* on April 7, 1895, to explain new rules for the use of the Union Gospel Tabernacle. After first saying that it had been abused "like all of God's blessings to mortal men," he went on to call for a banishment of politics from its pulpit. In the short run he succeeded in keeping politics out of the building, but in the long run the Auditorium served as a large and convenient forum for political debate and ceremony. Notable examples were the inauguration of Governor Austin Peay in 1923 and a rousing speech by Alfred E. Smith during the presidential campaign of 1928.

Symbolizing the secondary role which religious activities eventually took in the Auditorium's history were the deaths of the men who had built the auditorium and the effective change in the name of the building to mask its religious foundations. Tom Ryman himself had absolutely refused to countenance any re-naming of the building in his honor, but so popular was the desire to honor this son of Nashville by its citizens that upon his death they took matters out of the hands of his trustees.

Captain Ryman had been ill for several years but had withdrawn from his business affairs only shortly before his death in 1904. Confined to a wheelchair by injuries sustained in an accident between his carriage and a transport wagon, Ryman worsened in December and his health was headline news in

Nashville. He died quietly on December 23, and the city mourned his passing.

Sam Jones spoke to the thousands who attended his funeral in the Tabernacle. People from all walks of life, wealthy and poor alike, paid solemn respect to the man who in fact and by reputation had done so much for their city with his unostentatious charity. They saw the Tabernacle "both inside and out appropriately draped for the occasion" with black and white streamers as well as numerous American flags. Nashville's religious, business, and cultural leaders occupied the 100 seats on or near the stage with the river men Ryman had known throughout his life conspicuous in their grief.

Sam Jones choked back his tears with a tribute: "I go into the garden of my heart and pluck the rarest and sweetest flowers that ever blossomed there and lay them on his grave." At the conclusion of the eulogies, Jones suggested quietly that it would be appropriate to name the Tabernacle after the man who loved it so well. *The American* reported the overwhelming response: ". . . as one person the thousands who heard him were upon their feet." Immediately after the funeral, the steamboat men of Nashville reassembled in the Tabernacle and adopted a resolution calling for a change in the name of the building to the Ryman Auditorium.

In its edition the next day, the *Banner* reminded its readers that five years earlier Dr. Ira Landrith had made the same suggestion as a way of acknowledging the Captain. At the time Ryman modestly refused to hear such talk, but now, the *Banner* opined, there could be no more fitting monument to his memory. For many days following the funeral, various groups in Nashville published resolutions urging the new name. Their actions reflected not only respect for Tom Ryman but also indicated a belief that the Tabernacle belonged to the people of Nashville.

A poll by the *Banner* of the trustees found that a majority favored the resolution, but change was long in coming. Perhaps the strength of a reluctant minority or, more likely, legal complexities stymied the will of the public, for the official change did not occur until December 20, 1944, by Amendment to the Charter of Incorporation. For the people of Nashville, the Union Gospel Tabernacle became the Ryman Auditorium when they voted with their feet at the Captain's funeral. They have never wavered from their preference. In spite of another official name change in 1963, when the Tabernacle became the Grand Ole Opry House, Nashvillians have continued to refer to it affectionately as "the Ryman" to this day.

Only two years after the Captain's funeral, news of Sam Jones' death saddened Nashvillians. In a fitting departure, he was stricken while returning from a revival, and he died on October 15, 1906, in the sleeping car of the train taking him home to Cartersville, Georgia. Sam Jones' share in bringing the idea of a vast revival hall for all the people of Nashville to fruition had been in some ways as important as Ryman's. If Tom Ryman was the "Father of the Tabernacle," surely Sam Jones was its godfather.

_____

GREATE CONCERTE,

APRIL, XIII. *1905*

TO BE HOLDEN AT Ye

RYMAN AUDITORIUM,

(wh is fette downe in 5th Avenue.)

TICKETS - - 25 CENTS.

All ye money will go to ye Daughters of ye Confederacy.

Tennessee State Library and Archives

GREATE CONCERTE,

FRIDAY, NOVEMBER 24, 1922

TO BE HOLDEN AT Ye

RYMAN AUDITORIUM

(wh is fette downe in 5th Avenue.)

TICKETS - - - - 25 CENTS

All ye money will go to ye Andrew Jackson Society Fund

II. The Ryman:
Opera House and Theater

Even before the deaths of the two men responsible for building the Tabernacle, its maintenance and operation had been delegated to a group of civic-minded businessmen. In keeping with the expanded purposes to which the building was put, the State of Tennessee had granted a group of fifty representatives a new charter for the Union Gospel Tabernacle on May 11, 1901. This document expressed essentially the same goals as the earlier Articles, but it charged the trustees with the task of maintaining the Tabernacle in condition for public purpose. The new committee, whose president for its first three years was Tom Ryman, had raised enough money to lower the debt to $9,000, but its members still worried over the remainder.

To the end of reducing it further, Major E. B. Stahlman, owner-founder of *The Nashville Banner*, advised his fellow directors to cooperate with the Philharmonic Society of Nashville in its invitation to the Metropolitan Opera Company of New York to perform in the city. When the ladies of the Society realized that they could not guarantee even half of the $10,000 demanded by the opera company, the directors of the Tabernacle decided to go it alone. Since the Society had made the initial invitation, the ladies did not relinquish their interest in the event and were instrumental in its success. To ensure that the building's meager resources would not suffer, each of the "fifty representative citizens" guaranteed $200 of the Metropolitan's expenses.

But for the Metropolitan Opera to perform in Nashville the Ryman would have to have a stage. This problem, one which of necessity had to be solved quickly, would add considerably to the expense of bringing the company to Nashville. Nevertheless, the committee decided that the cost of $750, not to mention the loss of seats that lowered the auditorium's capacity to 3,574 people, was worth the potential benefit.

In 1901 a building committee oversaw construction of the new stage, while Nashville prepared for the only two performances by the Metropolitan Opera ever given in the city. The organizers spent heavily on advertisements and persuaded the railroads to offer special rates for the occasion. At $5 for the most expensive box seats and $1.50 for standing room, tickets for the opera did not come cheap.

Maurice Grau directed the 250-person company of the Metropolitan Opera during its national tour in 1901 with *Carmen*, *The Barber of Seville,* and *Faust*. The famed principals, Mmes. Calvé, Eames, and Sembrich, traveled apart from the regulars and went only to those cities where they would be performing. Ironically, the Union Gospel Tabernacle, the site of Nashville's holy reawakening, played host on its new stage to one of the most infamous women of easy virtue in literature, the feisty Carmen, but art conquers all. The trustees took careful note of her ability to elevate mankind, and even the newspapers glossed over the more unseemly conduct of this most amorous of heroines. Emma Calvé, the soprano who had created the role of Santuzza in *Cavalleria Rusticana* at its premiere, and one of the greatest singers in operatic history, was scheduled, but failed to perform as Bizet's naughty wench. For *The Barber of Seville*, the great Polish belcanto soprano Marcella Sembrich, whom Nashville audiences had already seen and admired with the Boston Festival Orchestra, was cast as Rosina.

In spite of a brouhaha over Emma Calvé's refusal to appear, the occasion was a gala one, with the auditorium divided into boxes for the wealthier patrons. *The American*'s critic, Ada Scott Rice, praised the thoughtfulness of the audience by noting that the women of Nashville deserved "canonization for the very general leaving of their hats at home." Yet fashion was served. Rice noted with satisfaction that "it was truly a metropolitan audience in the matter of elaborate dress. Appropriate evening dress was much more generally observed *than even at the recent horse show* [author's italics]."

The whole production won extravagant kudos from the Nashville press, but more important these two performances changed the cultural history of the city. Equipped with a stage large enough to present grand opera, the Tabernacle would continue to attract spectacular entertainment to Nashville. If Sam Jones, who was on a revival tour, remained calm while a slut, albeit a make-believe one, commanded his stage, legend has it that Captain Ryman railed enough for both of them. He supposedly installed himself at a lectern beneath the stage and fulminated against the ungodly spectacle going on above his head. He is said to have remained there throughout the four acts and preached without drawing breath. Though apocryphal, the story underscores a tension between secular and religious aims that persist to this day in American culture. Disputes over the proper uses of the Tabernacle would continue.

The Metropolitan's visit to the Ryman was a harbinger of a half-century of glamor. All the great stars of opera's golden age eventually played the Ryman. The event that foretold its future direction was the appearance in concert in 1904 of the greatest, certainly the most famous, singer of the nineteenth century in America after Jenny Lind: Adelina Patti, a woman whose singing was synonymous with vocal perfection.

Madame Patti first sang in Nashville in 1859, and by 1904 she had passed into opera legend. For twenty-three years she reigned supreme in Covent Garden, undeniably the idol at whose feet England's opera-loving audiences worshipped. In Nashville she sang not only the great arias for which she was celebrated but also a selection of the sentimental tunes which were popular at the time. Of course, she performed her famous rendition of "Home, Sweet Home," which was said to be so moving that it melted the hearts of wooden Indians. Unfortunately for Nashvillians, a janitor chose a moment midway through her song to shovel coal into the two big stoves at the front of the auditorium. The interruption disconcerted Madame Patti for only a moment; she overcame the noise by singing much louder.

This greatest of singers was a herald for the great opera stars who came to the Ryman after her. For the quantity and quality of musical events on its stage, the Ryman's history as a showcase of the great artists of opera's golden age is unrivaled. Other cities may have had more elaborate productions, but no other city boasted such a varied, rich schedule.

In its first twenty years the Ryman hosted an international Who's Who of musical artistry. The Czech pianist Ottokar Malek, the Australian coloratura soprano Nellie Melba, the Italian baritone Giuseppe Campanari, the French diva Emma Calvé, Indiana's Lillian Nordica, the impresario-singer Bessie Abbot and her company, and the "world's greatest violinist" Jan Kubelik. Mr. Kubelik shared his title with Jascha Heifetz and Mischa Ellman, both of whom came to the Ryman many times in their careers. Other great singers came and conquered Nashville: Emma Eames, Louise Homer, Ernestine Schumann-Heink, David Bispham, Mary Garden, Alessandro Bonci, and Luisa Tetrazzini. Marian Anderson performed in her turn, as did Lily Pons, Alma Gluck, Giovanni Martinelli, and John McCormack.

Two of the biggest names in opera appeared back-to-back in 1919. Amelita Galli-Curci, who played the Ryman several times, and Enrico Caruso, who only played it once, seemed to overlap with the noisy ovations they aroused, fanfares which echo still in the historic hall; the week they appeared in Nashville is often cited as the most glorious in the city's long musical tradition.

Fritz Kreisler openly admitted his admiration for the Ryman's acoustics, as did Vladimir de Pachman and Yehudi Menuhin. The Russian composer Rachmaninoff played tortured music in the auditorium, and, in 1908 the virtuoso pianist and celebrated composer Ignace Jan Paderewski made the first of many visits to the stage. From the beginning he lived up to his billing as the greatest pianist since Paganini, but he, like others before and after him, took exception to the rudeness of his audience. He walked off the stage, in mid-note as it were, when the noise of departing patrons distracted him during an encore. Chastened, those in a hurry to go to their carriages stood stock-still when the general applause coaxed him to return to the piano.

The touring opera companies came, the San Carlo in the twenties and Charles F. Wagner's in the thirties and forties. Great conductors brought their symphonies: Walter Damrosch and the New York Symphony Orchestra, Modest Altschuler and the Russian Symphony Orchestra, Eugene Ormandy and the Philadelphia Symphony Orchestra, and Victor Herbert and his orchestra. Band leaders came: Giuseppe Creatore, John Philip

Sousa, Paul Whiteman, Wayne King, Spike Jones, and Fred Waring.

Dancers introduced Nashville audiences to the new American ballet. Isadora Duncan demonstrated "free-form;" Ruth St. Denis shocked with her scanty costumes; the Polish Swan Anna Pavlova interpreted the classics; Ted Shawn and his Male Dancers set many a heart aflutter with their athletic interpretations; and Nijinsky danced for a very small audience under the watchful, jealous eye of Serge Diaghilev who stood in the wings. The touring companies brought the classics of ballet to Nashville: the Joos Ballet with *Coppelia*, Sadler Wells with *Les Sylphides*, the Ballet Russe of Monte Carlo with *Prince Igor*, and the American Ballet Theater in *Swan Lake*.

Madame Patti's visit to the auditorium back in 1904 started it all, but as far as the Ryman was concerned hers was not the only divine presence in the room that night. Seated in the auditorium and bedazzled for life was Mrs. Lula C. Naff, whose love affair with the Ryman, an attachment she herself dated from that night when Patti's voice resonated so splendidly in the hall, was to make it later one of the most famous houses for music and theater in the business.

By 1908 musicians were not the only performers to enjoy the famed acoustics of the Ryman. Nashville audiences had heard several distinguished speakers in the Ryman Auditorium. Besides evangelists, such notables as Carry Nation and Frances Willard had spoken out against strong drink. Lectures as diverse as Lorado Taft's on sculpture and Elbert Hubbard's on "The Work of the Roycrofters" had instructed Nashvillians in the fine arts. Local professors had taught everything from ethics and humor to crafts and engineering from the stage.

None, however, could have enjoyed the same reception as Nashville's most famous visitor of 1907. On October 27th, the city aired its "gala attire" for the next day's arrival of President Theodore Roosevelt. *The American* reported that the President was on his way in his special train, *Magnate*, and that "on the arrival of the Presidential [car] a salute of twenty-one guns will be fired from Capitol Hill in the President's honor. The salute will be a signal for the bells and whistles of the city to take up the work of announcing to the people of Nashville that the President has arrived." Advising further that the city had arrayed itself "in the gayest dress, perhaps of its entire history," the paper predicted that the crowds would "fill every available inch of the roped-in sidewalks, crowd every window on the line of march and pack every point of vantage from which the distinguished visitor may be seen."

The city had decked itself in bunting, rope, flags, and "teddy bears enough to stock a zoo." Paintings of scenes from the old Rough Rider's life decorated various intersections he would pass, the last one depicting him as "President" and hung from the roof of the Ryman. The papers urged those Nashvillians "on tiptoe with excitement" to get to the Auditorium early, for it was sure to be jam-packed for Roosevelt's address.

And it was. The President, buoyed by the contagious cheering he heard on the way to the Auditorium, stood up in his carriage the whole way and "was as full of enthusiasm as a college boy." The building was ablaze with color and noisy with welcome. The planners had taken great pains to segregate all Vanderbilt University students because of their reputation for raucous and boisterous behavior. They proved the organizers correct when the President expressed his admiration for their football team. So often was he interrupted by spontaneous salvos of "Bully" from the adoring crowd, he spoke longer than anticipated. Declaring himself delighted with his reception in Nashville, he spoke on the purposes of his trip, a study of the problems of the Mississippi Valley region and how best to implement reform and bring about economic prosperity.

After leaving the Auditorium, his entourage visited Vanderbilt and Peabody College, where the overjoyed students greeted him merrily with a special cheer:

Rah, rah, rah, rah, rah, rah
Teddy Bear, Teddy Bear
Boo oo-oo-oo

While at Andrew Jackson's home, the Hermitage, he charmed his hosts by the courtesy with which he accepted welcome from the former President's granddaughter, Mrs. Rachel Jackson Lawrence. She gave him a tour of the mansion and presented him with a hand-carved hickory stick. The gift must have been the occasion for his reported remark: "By George, this is the kind of stuff I like when I hunt bears." In farewell to the city, he vowed to return; with a final "so long" he left on *Magnate* to conquer other cities with his infectious good nature. The Ryman had served the city well on an historic occasion when its citizens cooperated in a rare display of public-spiritedness and municipal pride.

Other noted speakers followed him to the Ryman: the socialist Eugene V. Debs, the suffragette Sylvia Pankhurst, the founder of the Boy Scouts Sir Robert Baden Powell, the advocate for the blind Helen Keller (with Ann Sullivan Macy), First Lady Eleanor Roosevelt for the Girl Scouts, and famed aviator Eddie Rickenbacker.

Two of the great humorists of the twentieth century spoke in the Ryman. The beloved Will Rogers charmed the city with his appearances, and W. C. Fields must have mightily disturbed the Captain's ghost when he proclaimed on stage that the best cure for a hangover was the application to the throat and stomach of the juice of three bottles of whiskey.

Some who came to speak on behalf of various causes were better known as actors than as orators. Rudolph Valentino spoke out against the way the Hollywood studios manipulated his fellow actors. Francis X. Bushman and Beverly Bayne lent their support to the Nashville Red Cross' war work, as did Charlie Chaplin, Mary Pickford, and Douglas Fairbanks.

The Ryman's glittering roster of performers gave luster to Nashville's past as "The Athens of the South" and prepared the city for its future as "Music City, U.S.A." Early in its existence, the Ryman Auditorium was established as a first-rate venue for anyone—politician, orator, preacher, singer, pianist—who could judge the high quality of its sound. These and others found in that wooden, circular interior a perfect environment, where a whisper had the resonance of a shout, where a pianissimo sounded as clear as a fortissimo, in short, a natural theater for those hardy enough to endure its discomforts.

Although Nashville had seen two grand opera performances in the Auditorium, they had not yet seen a "grand" theatrical event. When news made the rounds that Sarah Bernhardt planned an appearance on March 8, 1906, theater lovers in the city considered it the cultural event of the young century for Nashville. Again, to accommodate the production and to avoid the problems of the past, the Board authorized Mr. J. Gordon Edwards to improve the stage by extending and squaring it off at front, thereby removing two sections of seats. In this way the stage was to have dressing rooms and storage cabinets, but Mr. Edwards apparently never got around to finishing them. From an

Pews, a naked light bulb, basins, and curtains marked the spot in the corner of the Ryman Auditorium where chorines (chorus girls) and dancers applied makeup while looking after the star's dog. Special Collections/Vanderbilt University Library

early photograph of a rehearsal in the Ryman, we know that the management used curtains to hide the dressing space and that the chorines actually put on their make-up in pews.

Arriving on a special railroad car designed just for her use, Sarah Bernhardt brought her entire Parisian company to Nashville. Before the end of her long, glorious career, she had toured the United States nine times, but the tour which brought her to Nashville in 1906 was the most unusual and billed as her last, one of many "farewell tours." She refused to accept the dictates of the Theatrical Syndicate and took her troupe to tents, schoolhouses, and other non-traditional playhouses. Her disagreement with the guild explains her appearance in the Ryman; normally she would have been booked into the Vendome Theater downtown.

Although sixty-one years old at the time, she nonetheless recreated her most famous role, the young, consumptive courtesan, Camille. According to the *Banner*, no more brilliant or larger audience, 3,140 people, had ever witnessed a dramatic event in Nashville. "The Divine Sarah," no longer young and never so beautiful as Dumas' tragic heroine, captivated the audience and held it spellbound with her embodiment of the pitiful, doomed demi-mondaine. Though speaking French, she used the "golden bell" of her voice and her magical talent for expressing physical agony to enthrall her audience with the sad tale of love lost, love regained and lost again. Tears of sympathy flowed when Mlle. Gautier died in Armand's arms. Bravos soon followed.

Such a theatrical event was not yet standard fare at the Ryman and would not become so until the thirties when Mrs. Naff began to make the auditorium "the most talked-about one-night stand on the road." Through the teens and twenties, such theater as there was in the Ryman consisted of touring Shakespearean companies.

The Ryman also saw lighter fare in the form of occasional Vaudeville performers. Sir Harry Lauder was a "big name" attraction, but no more so than Anna Held, whose famous snow-white bosom and diamond stockings titillated her audience at the Ryman. Vaudeville continued to come even after its heyday had passed, but the revues were modified into something like Broadway musicals. Mrs. Naff later brought *The High Lights of 1934*, Earl Carroll's *Vanities*, George White's *Scandals*, and the *Ziegfeld Follies* with Billie Burke, Fanny Brice, and Eve Arden in the company.

In fact, the Ryman could not avoid being touched by the most popular entertainment of the day. Movies marched relentlessly toward a quasi-monopoly on light entertainment, and even the old Tabernacle unrolled from time to time a homemade screen, a thick muslin sheet, primarily for early educational films. Of course the Ryman never became a movie palace, but one farsighted woman made it synonymous with legitimate theater for many years.

Until her retirement in 1955, Lula C. Naff, who preferred the more businesslike "L. C. Naff," was the acknowledged "high priestess of the Tabernacle." She never considered her "child," the Ryman, as a relic of a bygone era; rather, she saw it as a vital showplace, whose church-like interior deserved to be filled to overflowing with "congregations" worshipping at its dual altar of music and theater. She and the building she loved so well became in time the grand old ladies of Nashville's commu-

Lula C. Naff, "high priestess of the Ryman"
F. Robinson Collection/Vanderbilt University Library

nity of the arts, but her work did not stop at the borders of the city or even at those of the state of Tennessee. Each nurturing the other, she and the Ryman matured and grew famous together, both hot topics of conversation among "show folk" who visited.

When it was suggested to her that she worked too hard in

promoting the building, Mrs. Naff tartly responded that her labor kept her too busy to succumb to the high blood pressure and heart trouble which seemed to plague her less well-occupied friends. When she was finally forced by age to retire, Mrs. Naff complained that she was resting too much: "If they'd just give me the Ryman back with its dust and paint and a big block of tickets, I wouldn't ask anything else," she wrote to her friend Francis Robinson.

The building was her life, as she put it, and indeed it never had a more vigorous defender nor a more vociferous advocate. Whether from journalists, city councilmen, artists, or her own trustees, she allowed no criticism of the Ryman to go unanswered, no slight to go unremarked.

Born in 1875, Mrs. Naff moved to Nashville with the Delong Rice Lyceum Bureau as its secretary and bookkeeper in 1901. She was the booking agent for the Bureau in effect long before she had the job in fact, since the Rice Agency provided the lyceum course of popular entertainment for the Ryman until 1914. In that year, the indomitable Mrs. Naff, rather than find other work when the Bureau dissolved, leased the building on her own. For the next four years, she rented the Auditorium on an annual basis and by 1920 had shown herself so capable that the governing board reorganized around her.

Mrs. Naff realized from the beginning that the traditional lyceum mixture of moralizing lecturers and "light" entertainers was unable to draw sufficiently large audiences to make her venture worthwhile. As she put it, "Who wanted to hear Billy Sunday when they could go see Mary Pickford for a dime?" If a "star entertainer" was touring, she endeavored to attract him or her to the Ryman, and in such fashion she was able to bring to Nashville, in addition to those already mentioned, such artists as Rosa Ponselle, whose two trips were widely publicized; Geraldine Farrar, who had her own contingent of groupies, the Nashville Gerryflappers; and, the actors Walter Hampden and Fritz Lieber, who brought Shakespeare's plays to the stage. She also cooperated with various Nashville groups to bring in such musicians and singers as Arturo Rubinstein, Frieda Hempel, Maria Jeritza, Marion Talley, and Beniamino Gigli.

Numerous stories about the acerbic manager of the Ryman eventually circulated throughout the nation, but none gained more currency than her earliest "coup." Undaunted by the wariness of her advisors and firm in her resolve to bring the very best entertainers to the Auditorium, Mrs. Naff contracted with the opera singer John McCormack for his only southern appearance of the year 1916. His management demanded a guaranteed fee of $3,000, an amount most people would have considered prohibitively high for a city the size of Nashville.

To publicize the concert Mrs. Naff did not deny the widely circulated rumor that she had taken a second mortgage on her house to underwrite McCormack's performance. She repeated the story countless times in her later years, and it has become established as fact in Nashville. Knowing its value as publicity, Mrs. Naff gave the story new life when she again used it to announce McCormack's last appearance in the Ryman in the thirties: "There is no mortgage on the home, but again John McCormack, World's Greatest Lyric Tenor, will sing at Ryman Auditorium, Nashville, Monday evening, October 12, [1936]." The strategy worked, and the singer sold out the house one last time.

In spite of her brusqueness, Lula Naff was masterful in manipulating the media for the purpose of advertising events at the Ryman. She certainly was not above a little selective arrangement of the facts when she believed that the newspapers were ignoring her schedule. Many letters of congratulation from agents prove the contention that she was an "A-1 publicist." In the specific case of John McCormack's concert, she actually had only the original mortgage on her house at the time of the booking. In a letter in Francis Robinson's papers at Vanderbilt University, Mr. Littel Rust, her friend and attorney, revealed: "The McCormack concert of 1916 is history. Even though the story that she put a mortgage on her house is a good one, no mortgage was ever signed, and $3,000 was cleared on his performance."

Roy A. Miles, one of the last directors of the Ryman Corporation before the building was sold in 1963, also contradicted the legend in a speech to students at Vanderbilt University, while adding that "the appearance of John McCormack added tremendous prestige to the auditorium . . . ." Though there was no second mortgage, it is safe to say that Mrs. Naff was willing to bank everything on McCormack's appearance. And with good cause.

The great Irish tenor was a concert favorite throughout the

nation. McCormack had sung with major companies in Europe and the United States and in 1916 was between three-year stints with the Metropolitan Opera. Enrico Caruso was better-known but hardly more beloved than John McCormack. The sublime artistry of his phrasing, the exquisite purity of his voice, and the intuitive feeling of his characterizations made him an operatic legend, but it was for the ballads and folk songs of his native land that he was most revered. He was a genuinely popular man whose radio broadcasts were avidly followed by his thousands of fans. Certainly, his fame and appeal foretold success for Mrs. Naff's brash venture.

At first she may have had real cause for alarm. She worried about the lack of interest in the concert, but she sprang to action. As would remain her habit, she carried around handwritten publicity releases; she frantically put up posters, passed out handbills, and hawked her show on the streets.

She succeeded so well that three days before the tickets were to go on sale to the public, she found that she had none left, having already sold all the available seats by mail or through reservations. When she finally opened her office for the public sale, she found a block-long line of people waiting, and rather than refuse them places she sold standing-room seats, and, for a slightly higher price, seats on the stage itself.

When she finished, she found that she had sold over 5,000 tickets for a building which normally strained to admit 4,000. She later joked that some people had more confidence in her abilities to sell out the concert than she did: scalpers sold tickets at the door for $25 each. Mrs. Naff placed patrons in every available square inch of space. More than 300 ended up on the stage with John McCormack, for whom a narrow alley was left so that he could walk to the grand piano. The good-natured tenor turned his back on the thousands before him for one song so that he could sing directly to the hundreds forced to sit behind him.

After the concert, Mrs. Naff slyly maintained that she had made enough money to pay off both mortgages on her house with enough left to venture on other artists. No wonder that of all the many artists she introduced to Nashville, McCormack remained her favorite. In fact, she dated the real beginning of her career from his concert in 1916. She herself gave the best review of his performance: "But oh! it was wonderful . . . when he'd sing, it was the sweetest thing you ever heard—made you romantic enough to fall for it." High praise indeed from a woman known for her abruptness and no-nonsense approach to sentimentality.

After this triumph, Mrs. Naff went on to many others, but the concerts by McCormack, Galli-Curci, and Caruso made Nashville aware of a new spirit at the Ryman.

The board also realized that finally they had found the right manager for a building still carrying a debt of some $6,000. It was also badly in need of repairs as well as additional funds to sustain the world-class entertainment which Mrs. Naff had shown herself capable of booking.

According to the *Tennessean*, Bernard Fensterwald, a prominent Nashvillian, originated a plan whereby a new group of directors would lease the Auditorium for fifty years. This group formed an operating company, the Auditorium Improvement Company, "to underwrite the present mortgage of about $6,000, provide improvements to the building, including adequate heating and lighting systems, decorations, improved sanitation, and other means to render the building safe and . . . to assume the costs of ordinary repairs and insurance."

The new board, composed of some of Nashville's most distinguished business and professional men, agreed to contribute $15,000 to pay off the mortgage and to use for the noted improvements. They in turn were to be repaid from the Ryman's gate receipts. Wisely, they hired Mrs. Naff as the manager of the Ryman. She proved in short order that their faith was not misplaced: she paid off the $15,000 note within the next three years and never operated a single year with a loss.

The new Charter, issued September 20, 1920, declared that the Auditorium Improvement Company was "operated without profit to any individual, for the improvement of this building and for the better education and amusement of the people of Nashville." While the references to moral elevation and religious functions were gone, the Charter remained essentially faithful to the ideals of social philanthropy popularized in the city by Sam Jones.

Thus the Naff decades saw great changes in the Ryman's schedule and in the very building itself. Most important, the Auditorium became a legendary one-night stand for some of the greatest names in American stage history.

In those golden years of theater before radio and movies, the

A view of the Ryman interior from the Confederate Gallery.
Special Collections/Vanderbilt University Library

"Road" had been a lucrative source of revenue for troupes large and small, famous and unknown, good and bad. In those days Nashville had been a "dog-town," one in which plays were tried out "on the dog" before they moved to the supposedly more sophisticated New York City. The Ryman's astute manager looked around in 1931 and noted that her building was the only one large enough to offer legitimate theater; all the others had been virtually eliminated or converted into movie houses.

Other commentators had already declared the "Road" a dead-end, the "dog" without any bite, and legitimate theater itself a cadaver. Some even questioned why first-rate dramatic productions needed to go into the boondocks in the first place, once there only to suffer poor houses and cultural ignorance. Better to give the provinces a steady diet of Shakespeare's proven standards and an occasional vaudeville revue. Most of these same people generally placed the blame for the sad state of affairs squarely at the doorstep of the motion picture studios. Films had robbed the legitimate stage of its vitality, they argued, and it would better serve those loyal followers in the large urban centers if it stayed away from the hinterlands' fickle, ignorant public.

A local, wildly popular production of La Cavalleria Rusticana *held in the Ryman in 1927.* F. Robinson Collection/ Vanderbilt University

Mrs. Naff proved all these doomsayers dead wrong. Dismissing such arguments as uninformed, she made Nashville one of the earliest and most profitable stops on the slowly reviving "Road," even during the worst times of the Great Depression and the Second World War.

Mrs. Naff had three criteria for the shows she sought to book. First of all, she knew that she could overcome the waning public enthusiasm for theater by bringing in big stars. Over the next thirty years, she brought in Irene Castle, Gertrude Lawrence, Katharine Cornell, Maurice Evans, Alfred Lunt and Lynn Fontanne, Bela Lugosi, Clifton Webb, Judith Anderson, Walter Huston, Eva LeGallienne, Everett Marshall, Joe E. Brown, Melvyn Douglas, Harpo Marx, and Mae West. At the time of their Ryman debuts, some actors had yet to make "big-name" status: Doris Day, Tyrone Power, ZaSu Pitts, Orson Welles, Ann Blyth, Basil Rathbone, and Ethel Waters, among others.

Second, Mrs. Naff believed that she could sell out the house without a "name" in the cast, if the play itself was of recognized quality to assure general interest. Thus she presented *Strange Interlude*, *Mister Roberts*, *The Student Prince*, *Brother Rat* (with

Showbills tout appearances by stage divas Ethel Barrymore and Tallulah Bankhead. Nashville Room/Nashville-Davidson County Public Library

Eddie Bracken and Gary Merrill), and *Oklahoma*. One of these, *Tobacco Road*, which came twice to Nashville, caused Mrs. Naff to go to court to prevent the municipal authorities from censoring it.

Third, and the best possible alternative, was the "big play" with the "big stars." Such vehicles were a mainstay of Mrs. Naff's seasons and included Tallulah Bankhead in *Reflected Glory* and *The Little Foxes*, Helen Hayes in *Mary of Scotland* and *Victoria Regina*, Paul Lukas in *Watch Along the Rhine*, Colleen Moore in *Cindy*, and Ethel Barrymore in *Whiteoaks* and *The Love Duel*. Possibly the best example was Mrs. Naff's presentation of *The Philadelphia Story* in 1941, a performance Minnie Pearl thinks the most memorable of the non-Opry events in the Ryman's history. The cast included Katharine Hepburn, Van Heflin, and Joseph Cotten and played before a standing-room-only house.

Mrs. Naff, of course, did not have a full schedule of theater every year; in fact, some years, particularly in the fifties, the stage offered slim pickings for the fastidious Mrs. Naff. She "filled in" her schedule with appearances by such diverse artists as Lily Pons, the Ink Spots, Fritz Kreisler, Alicia Alonso, Lauritz Melchior, Patrice Munsel, Dorothy Lamour, Victor Borge, and Pete Fountain. Martha Graham and José Greco brought their dance companies. Gene Autry may have had bigger box office receipts, but Roy Rogers delighted Nashville's children by bringing along Dale Evans and Trigger. The Ted Mack Amateur Hour held its program in the Ryman in 1952. Yma Sumac tested the acoustics and raised the roof with her high-pitched warbling. The famous and not-so-famous jockeyed for position on the Ryman's busy schedule of local events, speakers, church meetings, and Opry performances.

The Ryman, however, was known nationally as a must-stop on the road for theatrical companies, especially after Brock Pemberton, famous for his writings on the state of contemporary theater, gave it national attention in an article of 1939. He called it "one of the most unusual" showplaces in the nation, and he named Mrs. Naff "the most picturesque manageress" in the business. Katharine Cornell and Alexander Woollcott also spread the fame of the Ryman with humorous anecdotes about the idiosyncratic Mrs. Naff and her Tabernacle-turned-play-house.

Of course, the old Tabernacle had not been designed for major stage productions, and it had changed little since the stage was enlarged to give Sarah Bernhardt room enough to expire in tubercular spasms. Others were afraid that the dusty, unsanitary backstage area might cause them a similar, unapplauded end. The "arrangements" were primitive and rudimentary, and even the stage itself was really insufficient for such large-scale spectacles as *Mary of Scotland*.

While opera divas may have been content to put on their make-up in screened pews, and Valentino himself may not have complained about dressing in a curtained-off corner, actors were not so eager to suffer such hardships for the sake of a one-night stand. Ethel Barrymore brought her own portable dressing room, a canvas cubicle no bigger than a phone booth. When the story spread that Miss Barrymore retreated to her little dressing room to engage in secret her habit of tippling between Acts I and II, Mrs. Naff had to scotch the rumor.

The great actress Maude Adams was not as hardy as Miss Barrymore. She might have had to fly around dusty rafters as Peter Pan earlier in her career—and had done so at least twice in

Nashville—but now that she was older and justifiably celebrated as a theatrical institution, she brooked no unnecessary discomfort. Just as Mrs. Naff was ready to sign the contract for the appearance of Miss Adams and Otis Skinner in their revival of *The Merchant of Venice* in 1932, she received a telegram from the star's manager informing her that as she had just learned that there was no running water in the dressing room backstage, Miss Adams would not appear. Little did Miss Adams know that were it not for her hasty cable she would not even have had a dressing room. Mrs. Naff had a space built according to her specifications, a roomlet which, ironically, later became the exclusive property of the male stars of the Opry. But for a little while, women had a serviceable rest room, thanks to Maude Adams.

Helen Morgan, the torch singer who came in 1936, found Miss Adam's legacy to her fellow troupers, the dressing room, unbearably cold. Maintaining that she could hardly sing through chattering teeth, she dispatched her unlucky manager to find a portable heater, even though all the stores downtown had already closed for the day. He finally found one in the nick of time, and a warmed Miss Morgan sang her sultry tunes.

Fanny Brice appeared in Billy Rose's *Crazy Quilt* before Maude Adams had raised the ruckus over the dressing room. The famous comedienne may have suffered inconvenience, but she certainly had her priorities straight. Even on the day of her performance, she remained unaware that female members of shows had to dress in a small, cramped bathroom off the lobby, truly a "water closet" in every sense of the phrase. Miss Brice's manager delayed telling her until the last minute. Finally, after working up his nerve, he approached the lady and began: "Miss Brice, I want to tell you that you have to dress in..."

"Never mind where I have to dress, how is the house?" she snapped.

Hoping to dodge a bullet, the gentleman happily replied, "It's better than $3,500."

"Och, for a $3,500 house, I'd dress in a [expletive deleted]."

"Well," he interrupted "that's exactly where you are dressing!"

Crazy Quilt, a rowdy, uproarious comedy, was the subject of a vehement condemnation by the preacher at the old First Presbyterian Church downtown. Imagine his rage when, on another occasion, a very famous actress drunkenly stumbled into his vestry. Knowing only that she was to play in a big, old church in

Nashville, the potted thespian chose the first one she came across and demanded the astonished reverend's help in finding her dressing room. The story went that the good gentleman roused himself from his shocked stupor to reply, "Madame, you are dreadfully mistaken."

"This ish a church, ain't it?," she supposedly slurred. Assuring her it was, but not the one she sought, he sent her on her unsteady way to the Ryman, where Mrs. Naff did not refuse the sanctuary of *her* church.

Two other actresses caused headlines while in Nashville. Tallulah Bankhead held court in the tiny backstage area after one appearance and alternately charmed and shocked the fans and reporters who crowded around her. Later, after another appearance at the Ryman, she interrupted a cocktail party at the home of a local society leader; angered by what she believed was vindictive upstaging by her hostess, Miss Bankhead turned a hose on her and the other guests.

On March 30, 1938, during a stirring performance by Helen Hayes in *Victoria Regina*, the first lady of the American theater strode to the edge of the stage to deliver lines. Behind her the cast froze in their places when suddenly a curtain ripped from its moorings and, narrowly missing the star, dumped years of accumulated dust and debris on the cast. But with regal aplomb, Miss Hayes continued to chew the scenery.

Because of its history, its staff, and even its appearance, the Ryman often became a target. Writing in 1935, Herbert Drake for the *New York Herald Tribune* spiced his account of Fanny Brice's performance in the Ryman with a few words about the primitive hall and its immoderately eccentric manager. Mrs. Naff never forgave him either slight and later blamed his article for inspiring the patronizing comments in the actress Katharine Cornell's autobiography. Miss Cornell recalled that on her visits she watched Mrs. Naff distribute tickets from a shoebox (it was actually a shirtbox) on the streets of Nashville. She said that Mrs. Naff snacked on bananas as she walked the streets selling tickets, and whenever someone asked for a ticket, she found it "perhaps in the box, but more likely in her hair, or her cuff, or her sweater pocket." In 1958 Tyrone Power gave a press conference after a performance in the Ryman and criticized the city for not having an adequate theater for actors to practice their craft. Others such as Amelita Galli-Curci, Fritz Kreisler, and John

McCormack, praised the acoustics without dwelling on the discomforts.

Bob Hope brought Doris Day and the Les Brown Band with him in 1949 and broke all records for attendance and receipts at the Ryman. The comedian opened his show by announcing "What an amazing garage this is! What time do the bats fly out?" Describing the building as an intimate old place, he asked if he could have it when it fell down, but he begged the management not to take off the Band-Aids until he had gotten out. The place had had a great history; in fact, so many "longhairs" had played there that Bing Crosby would feel right at home.

Hope enjoyed his experience so much that the next day from New York he issued a press release gently poking fun at "America's most picturesque institution." Retelling the story about Captain Ryman pouring all his liquor into the Cumberland at the time of his conversion, Hope said, "Les Brown's Band heard about it and before we could stop them, they had on their diving trunks."

What Hope had to say about Nashville's famed Ryman enjoyed wide circulation: "It's [the Ryman] also Katharine Cornell's favorite theater and the audiences sure do love her. In fact, before I stepped out on the stage, they were laying 8 to 5 I'd never make as good a Juliet as she."

"In 1914 Mrs. Elsie [sic] Naff, the manager, mortgaged her home to bring John McCormack here. Of course, in those days she could have gotten Crosby for the same money."

"I wondered what all those ropes were on the stage for. Then I found out that when Caruso sang here, before he got the first note out, they had to fasten the building down."

"And I loved working [there]. The first balcony almost completely circles the theater and it's wonderful to have the audience all around you. Naturally every now and then I got that trapped feeling."

"But it was really a sellout and people were sitting on anything they could find. One woman complained when the manager gave her something to sit on. Halfway through the show she discovered it was her husband."

A program release announces the Opry's move to the
Ryman Auditorium. Although the year "1943" has been
added by a librarian and not printed on the release (upper left
corner), the date is correct according to the sequence of releases in the collection. WSM Special Collection/Vanderbilt University
Library

III. The Opry House

The Grand Ole Opry was connected to the Ryman Auditorium even before making its home there. On November 28, 1925, in the fifth floor of the National Life and Accident Insurance Company, the new radio station WSM ("We Shield Millions") was on the air. Two men, one seated, the other standing, shared the station's only microphone. At 8 p.m., George D. Hay announced himself as "The Solemn Old Judge" and introduced the first guest on the new WSM Barn Dance. The featured performer that night was an eighty-year-old fiddler, Uncle Jimmy Thompson, who boasted that he could "fiddle the taters off the vine."

Others thought so too. Uncle Jimmy Thompson had just won the Ford-sponsored regional Fiddlers' Contest held in the Ryman Auditorium. Since 1902 at least, "Old Fiddler Contests" had been held annually in the Auditorium, and "the wizard of the violin," as the newspapers called Uncle Jimmy, was a perennial winner. This "Champion Fiddler of Dixie" claimed that he knew over a thousand tunes, songs like "Leather Breeches," "Sleepy Lou," and "The Arkansas Traveler," but Judge Hay restricted him to an hour's worth on that fateful night in 1925. Uncle Jimmy supposedly complained, "Hell, I'm only getting warmed up after an hour." Before his time was up, telegrams were pouring into the station requesting that he play listeners' favorites.

The Barn Dance quickly became a sensation, but it was not the only program on Saturday nights. WSM, owned by National

Life and a member of the National Broadcasting Company network, also carried a classical program, "The Music Appreciation Hour." Its conductor was Dr. Walter Damrosch, the celebrated leader of the New York Symphony and acknowledged as one of the foremost interpreters of Wagner in the world. Nashville had already heard him conduct several times, and always in the Ryman Auditorium. His orchestra had been one of the earliest to perform in the newly-completed Tabernacle in the 1890s, and he was well-known to the people of Nashville. WSM's Barn Dance, now expanded to three hours, followed Dr. Damrosch's program on the schedule.

By 1927 the Solemn Old Judge was accustomed to following the "fine lace" of Dr. Damrosch's hour, as Hay called it, with the "homespun cloth" of his Barn Dance. In his memoir on the Opry, he recalled speaking the words that changed the course of American music:

"The monitor in our Studio B was turned on, so that we would have a rough idea of the time which was fast approaching. At about five minutes before eight, your reporter called for silence in the studio. Out of the loudspeaker came the correct, but accented voice of Dr. Damrosch and his words were something like this: 'While most artists realize there is no place in the classics for realism, nevertheless I am going to break one of my rules and present a composition by a young composer from Iowa, who sent us his latest number, which depicts the onrush of a locomotive. . . .'"

After the composition Dr. Damrosch signed off, and Judge Hay was on the air: "We paid our respects to Dr. Damrosch and said something like this: 'Friends, the program which just came to a close was devoted to the classics. Dr. Damrosch told us that it was generally agreed that there is no place in the classics for realism. However, from here on out for the next three hours we will present nothing but realism. . . . It will be down to earth for the earthy.'"

He then introduced DeFord Bailey, who played his train imitation, the "Pan American Blues," on the harmonica. After he had finished, Judge Hay stepped to the microphone and uttered words that still reverberate in the national musical consciousness: "For the past hour we have been listening to music taken largely from Grand Opera, but from now on we will present 'The Grand Ole Opry.'" Thus WSM found an "official" name for the program that has continued uninterrupted every Saturday night since 1925.

WSM also had a growing hit. When fans grew so numerous as to block the corridors, Edwin W. Craig, an official with National Life, suggested letting them into the studio. Not only would this free the halls but the crowd's enthusiasm would add to the program's immediacy. Hoping to turn a problem into a boon, National Life built Studio "C" to hold five hundred spectators. Before long, however, officials of the insurance company were complaining that so many people spilled out of the studio-auditorium to clog the corridors that their offices were almost unreachable.

In the thirties the Opry began a series of moves that led it first to the Hillsboro Theater, a location which quickly proved inadequate for the crowds who wanted to see the show. The Opry packed up and moved across the Cumberland to the old Dixie Tabernacle on Fatherland Street in east Nashville. There spectators shuffled through the sawdust on the floor to sit on rough, splintery benches to hear such groups as The Fruit Jar Drinkers and The Gulley Jumpers and to watch the antics of Sallie and Sairie. Some of the luckier ones were there the night a young man from East Tennessee, Roy Acuff, appeared with his Smoky Mountain Boys and sang "The Great Speckled Bird."

The homeowners in the otherwise quiet neighborhood eventually demanded that the Opry take its parking problems, its raucous patrons, and its loud music elsewhere; so the Opry moved out of the Dixie Tabernacle in 1939.

Its next home was the War Memorial Auditorium, a relatively new hall in downtown Nashville directly across from the National Life Building. Roy Acuff recalled that he and his band would tune up and dress in the WSM building and then walk across to the Auditorium when it was time to perform. WSM decided that it had to control the crowds in some way and began charging a twenty-five-cent entrance fee for the first time in 1939. But the fans still came in greater and greater numbers, and Opry announcer Grant Turner said, "they brought with them their chewing tobacco and gum and pocket knives to leave their initials in the War Memorial's fine leather seats." Three thousand and more came each week, and the wear-and-tear on the Auditorium led to a polite but firm request that the Opry find another home.

Precisely when this happened has been a controversy. Roy Acuff admitted, "I don't remember the year exactly, but some say it was '41 and some '43." Others distinctly remember Opry performances in the Ryman even before 1940. Yet, in newspaper accounts, in histories of Nashville and Tennessee, and even in some of the literature about the Opry put out by souvenir sellers, the exact date of the move to the Ryman Auditorium is often given as 1941. In an interview before he died in 1988, Mr. Herman Crook distinctly remembered The Crook Brothers first performing at the Ryman in 1941. Mr. Lewis Crook concurs: "I am positive that it was in 1941, because I left for the service before it left the War Memorial, and when I came home it was in the Ryman Auditorium."

Minnie Pearl distinctly recalled the date as 1942: "We had a soldier show for the Selective Service in 1941 called The Camel Caravan where we were sent around to the camps by the R. J. Reynolds Tobacco Company, which was one of the sponsors of the network portion of the Opry, to distribute cigarettes and promote their products. At that time, I was just doing the straight radio program, not the network. In 1942 the Camel Caravan was in Jacksonville, Florida, and Mr. Harry Stone, who managed the Opry came down there and told me, 'Minnie, they're going to put you on the network section next Saturday.' So, I went on in 1942, and the night I got there, I remember very vividly that one of the old sandbags which hung down from the ceiling in the Ryman Auditorium hit me in the head. I was just starting on stage, and they were changing the scenery from whatever show preceded the network show. So, I don't know exactly how long we were there, but, from having that sandbag hit me, I know we were there in 1942. It doesn't matter really, but I do know that I began with the Opry in 1940 in the War Memorial Building, and, by the way, the War Memorial doesn't have any sandbags."

One possible source for some of the confusion is an article by F. B. Gillis in the December 1956 issue of *Country & Western Jamboree*: "The scene of the country shenanigans hopped from the WSM Studio, to the Ryman Auditorium to the War Memorial Auditorium and back to the Ryman not only because it is the biggest place in Nashville but the barn-like structure adds atmosphere to the proceedings." Saying "Ryman" for the first move when he meant the "Dixie," Gillis probably

Roy Acuff celebrates his 59th birthday at the Ryman in 1962 with onlookers (left-right) Hank Snow, Ira Louvin, Charlie Louvin, Ott Devine, and David Cobb. Grand Ole Opry Archives

confused his tabernacles.

Historians at the Country Music Foundation, as well as present-day management of Opryland USA Inc, however, are emphatic that the move occurred in 1943. They may not have had sandbags fall on their heads, but they have documentary and circumstantial evidence on their side.

A short article in the *Tennessean* on June 5, 1943, stated: "The Grand Ole Opry, Saturday night radio show of Station WSM, will be staged hereafter at Ryman Auditorium, starting tonight, instead of at the War Memorial Building as previously, it was announced yesterday by Harry Stone, station manager." In addition, among Vanderbilt University's library special collections, a program release from May 30 to June 13, 1943, announces: "Now . . . Grand Ole Opry moves to Ryman Auditorium. Now there will be room for them [spectators] and additional hundreds in Ryman Auditorium." The release illustrates six army trucks with the words "Grand Ole Opry," and says, "The Opry is 17 years old and still growing!"

Finally, a contract that National Life signed with the Auditorium Improvement Company to lease the "Ryman Auditorium to

Ernest Tubb signs autographs for fans in the balcony that curves into the backstage area. Grand Ole Opry Archives

the Grand Old Opery [*sic*] for 52 consecutive Saturday nights" began on June 5, 1943, with National Life paying $100 per Saturday night, exempting one night in November from the lease because of a prior concert commitment. Mrs. Naff's correspondence contains no mention of the Opry until after 1943 when she began to complain to her friend Francis Robinson that country music fans had begun blocking her doorways. She also reported to the Ryman's Board on July 29, 1943, that the Auditorium had been rented to WSM for fifty-two consecutive weeks at a rate of $100 a week—the first mention of WSM or the Opry in the extant minutes.

Another piece of circumstantial evidence is found in the Opry career of Ernest Tubb, who made his first appearance in December 1942 at the War Memorial Auditorium.

How did the date 1941 become commonplace in the literature for the move to the Ryman? Some point fingers at Judge Hay as the culprit, but in his history of the Opry he mentions no specific date, saying only: "Finally we moved the show to the Ryman Auditorium, the largest house in Middle Tennessee, where we now turn away audiences week after week." Nevertheless, the error, once made, went uncorrected in article after article until widely accepted. Neither Minnie Pearl, Roy Acuff, nor Curly Rhodes of Pee Wee King's Golden West Cowboys recall any performances in the Ryman before the official move, and it seems unlikely that the Opry moved from the Ryman to the War Memorial and back again.

June 5, 1943, however, was not the first time that country music had been heard in the Ryman. Not only had the Old Fiddlers' Contest been held there annually, having been postponed one time much to the annoyance of its sponsors because an opera production was held over, but Uncle Dave Macon had played there as well. Fiddling Sid Harkreader told Garrison Keillor all about it for an article in *The New Yorker* (May 6, 1974): "It has been reported in the newspapers,' he said dryly, 'that I claim to be the first fiddler who ever played the Grand Ole Opry. That is not true. Uncle Jimmy Thompson was. What I said was—and you take this down—I said that I was the first fiddler to play on WSM. That was shortly before Judge Hay started the Opry, on November 28, 1925.'"

Fiddling Sid had not finished setting the record straight: "I was also the first country musician from Tennessee to make a commercial recording in New York, along with Uncle Dave Macon. That was on July 12, 1924. We made eighteen sides for Vocalion. Uncle Dave and me were also the first country musicians to play here in the Ryman Auditorium. We played here on December 19, 1925." Perhaps he didn't count the old-time fiddlers as pure "country" musicians.

The move to the Ryman coincided with an event which Harry Stone, longtime station manager of WSM, called one of the "things which more firmly established Country Music as a form of entertainment than anything else." The sale of a portion of the Grand Ole Opry to the R. J. Reynolds Tobacco Company for broadcast over a regional network of NBC had provided the Opry with a powerful sponsor in the winter of 1938-39. On October 9, 1943, that program, the thirty minutes devoted to endorsing Prince Albert Smoking Tobacco and now originating from the Ryman, expanded from 63 to 129 stations in a coast-to-coast NBC hookup. The Ralston Purina Company, impressed by the success of Prince Albert, contracted that same year to sponsor another thirty minutes through stations affiliated with NBC in the South and Southwest. Thus in the very year of its move into the Auditorium, the Opry spread the name "Ryman" nationwide.

Four years later WSM's representative before the FCC Clear Channel hearing argued that the station's 50,000 watts "should not be curtailed." In defense of the station, he characterized "the Opry's tremendous enterprise" and gave a good description of what the move into the Ryman had entailed:

"Far beyond our original plans for the program, the Grand Ole Opry has become a national insitution. Let me briefly illustrate what I mean. We rent on an annual basis the largest auditorium in Middle Tennessee, in which we have installed complete studio facilities (control room, rehearsal rooms, public address system, floodlights, stage props, etc.). To handle the enormous crowds, we employ thirty-seven firemen, policemen, ushers, ticket sellers, stage hands and electricians. This number, added to the number of performers, gives us a total of one hundred fifty-two people in all. The talent costs alone on the Grand Ole Opry is [sic] $1500 per week."

The Ryman had 3,574 seats, but not all of them could be used because the pillars obstructed sight lines to the stage. The *Tennessean* reported in an article three weeks after the move into the Ryman that, large as it was the Ryman might not be big enough for the fans who "formed in lines more than a block long a hour and a half before the opening."

The War Memorial Auditorium seated roughly 2,200 people. With the move into the Ryman the Opry now afforded another thousand or so an opportunity to see the show each Saturday night. Minnie Pearl noted a direct correlation between the move to the Ryman and the "beginning of the explosion of country music." She cited the tent shows, which had begun to carry Opry stars to hamlets and villages throughout the South and Midwest in 1940 as one of the reasons for the explosion. "I was aware that things had changed when we moved into the Ryman," she said and gave two other reasons for that change from a popular show to a national sensation. Since the move occurred during wartime and more and more soldiers made up its audience in the Ryman, the Opry took on new meaning for thousands of homesick, sometimes frightened young men.

Times were propitious for spreading country music, and that is just what those soldiers did with their guitars and memories of nights at the Ryman.

In addition, Minnie Pearl thought that the Opry was successful in attracting outstanding talent to add to its already glittering roster. Uncle Dave Macon, the Opry's first big star, and Roy Acuff, the Opry's newest and brightest star, both moved into the Ryman along with the show. Others on those wartime programs included Bill Monroe, Ernest Tubb, Pee Wee King, Eddy Arnold, and Minnie Pearl as the only woman in the show. Roy Acuff's mounting fame through personal appearances on the road and through his movie roles fed the flames of the Opry's renown. As he said, "I didn't miss appearing on the Opry if I could help it. I just had to get in here for that Saturday night Opry. I would like to play somewhere like Myrtle Beach, South Carolina, on a Friday and be in here on Saturday. I'd get in here maybe three or four o'clock in the afternoon, and go right on to the Auditorium, and my wife would meet me with my clothes, and I'd leave after the Opry and go back on the road."

What Minnie Pearl called "the heightened excitement of the Opry in the Ryman" was due to changes in its lists of entertainers. The Opry was continuing its process of evolution from the stage of a former tabernacle, whose pews and arched windows became colorful descriptions in the hands of the national reporters who began showing up regularly to report on "folk" music. An article in *Colliers* magazine in 1951 led to a spate of others. "Thar's Gold in Them Thar Hillbilly Tunes," by Bill Davidson, chronicled the phenomenal growth in the Opry and its effect on Nashville. Others followed as out-of-town papers and magazines took note of the curious sight of "rustic" performers delighting thousands with their music and antics in an "old church." Through such articles, many of these entertainers became household names in the United States and enjoyed money as well as fame.

For his time Bob Wills and his Texas Playboys was such an act. His song "San Antonio Rose" was the best-selling record of 1939, and it was a foregone conclusion that he would eventually appear at the Opry. One of his guest appearances caused an incident which Minnie Pearl described best:

"Bob Wills was young and handsome in that devil-may-care sort of way. When he did all that Texas hollering, that 'Ahhaaa', some of the ladies would go all to pieces. He was the first person to park a bus in front of the Ryman, and what a sight they were coming out of it. He and the Playboys and San Antonio Rose all dressed in white cowboy outfits. Well, as you know, the Ryman has that semicircular balcony that curves around over the wings of the stage, and one of the ladies up there could not control herself when she saw Bob Wills. She stood up, started to shout, and fell out of the balcony directly onto the stage—a real showstopper since they had to stop and pick her up."

She said that retelling the story reminded her of a routine she did with Rod Brasfield, who told her, "Miss Minnie, I shot my dog."

"Why?" asked Minnie, "Was he mad?"

"Well, he wasn't very happy about it."

So, when people asked her if the lady who fell out of the balcony was hurt by the fall, Miss Minnie always answered, "Well, it didn't help her any."

Bob Wills, however, had as much impact on the Opry as his overenthusiastic fan had on its stage. He brought his electrified fiddles with him, an innovation which caused Judge Hay to have heartburn and which caused Roy Acuff to tell Minnie Pearl, "They goin' to ruin the Opry." But in actuality, electric guitars had already invaded the Ryman when the Golden West Cowboys and Ernest Tubb and the Texas Troubadours used them. One other story persists about Wills' appearance. It has been repeated widely that he brought the first snare drum onto the stage but that Opry officials made him hide it behind a curtain. Actually, Pee Wee King's group probably was the first to use drums at the Opry, but whether they were first hidden and then banished remains in question.

In an interview with Chet Hagan for his history of the Opry, E. W. Wendell, the chief executive officer of Opryland USA Inc, called the story about hiding the drums another of the "old tales around here." He said further that as long as the Opry remained at the Ryman, "only a stand-up snare drum was used because you couldn't fit a whole set of drums on the stage."

The issue of electrical instruments and drums has not gone away, but persists even today when they are standard sights in the new Opry House. Herman Crook scorned those who used them, and Roy Acuff still thinks they are "too loud" and "not pure."

New names began to be heard at the Opry after its move to the Ryman. In 1944 Lester Flatt joined Bill Monroe's bluegrass band. Also, as Minnie Pearl recalled fondly, Rod Brasfield joined the Ralston Purina network program that year; Whitey Ford, the Duke of Paducah, appeared as the comic on the Prince Albert program. Brasfield got a rousing ovation after his first performance at the Ryman due, Minnie Pearl said, to his "natural comedic talent. There was this little man on the stage with his suit too big and his hat mashed up in his pants and his rubber face telling jokes with perfect timing. Working with Rod those ten years in the Ryman is one of the most wonderful things that ever happened to me."

Other acts joined in 1945—the Bailes Brothers, Bradley Kincaid, Lew Childre, and Cowboy Copas, while Bill Monroe put together the group of musicians that one music historian has called the best five-piece band ever. In December of that year Earl Scruggs joined the Bluegrass Boys, and with him on banjo, Lester Flatt on guitar, Chubby Wise on fiddle, Howard Watts ("Cedric Rainwater") on bass, and Bill Monroe on mandolin and lead vocal, that band became the standard by which others have been measured. Fittingly, one of the last big festivals held in the Ryman Auditorium before the Opry moved out was a bluegrass "revival" in 1973 headlined by none other than Bill Monroe.

In late April of 1946, Red Foley, who brought along a young guitar player named Chet Atkins, took over the Prince Albert Show. The Willis Brothers and Lonzo and Oscar also joined the Opry in 1946. Eddy Arnold with his "pop" vocalizations brought a new sound to the stage. Grandpa Jones signed on in 1947, the year that also saw Opry entertainers for the first time in Washington's Constitution Hall and New York's Carnegie Hall, an occasion which prompted Ernest Tubb's often repeated remark about the latter room, "This place'd hold a lot of hay." The contrast between the grandeur of Carnegie Hall and the Ryman's rough-hewn hominess was not lost on country performers, who, according to Minnie Pearl, began to appreciate the tradition and warmth of the Ryman Auditorium.

In 1948 George Morgan came in to replace Eddy Arnold in the roster, and Minnie Pearl and Rod Brasfield teamed up on the Prince Albert Show with routines which would delight audiences for years. Little Jimmy Dickens remembered that his first night at the Ryman was also in 1948: "Roy Acuff brought me to the Opry. The one thing I remember most about my first appearance at the Ryman was my lifelong dream of just going backstage. I had been in radio in different parts of the United States for ten years before I first came to the Opry as a guest, and I thought that I was ready for it until I stepped on the stage of the Ryman Auditorium. I realized how many greats had stood there, and wondered whether or not I was worthy to follow them, and my knees started knocking, and I felt like I was doing my first talent contest even though I had ten years' experience. The Ryman Auditorium has a feel about it that's different from any stage I've ever been on in my forty to fifty years as an entertainer. I don't know what it is, but there's just something about the Ryman Auditorium."

Roy Acuff ran for governor of Tennessee in 1948, and WSM began its Friday night version of the Opry, the *Frolics,* in its studios. However, in 1949 the biggest event in country music occurred on the Ryman's stage. The night of June 11, 1949, may have seemed like just another night at the Opry for the thousands of fans and the people who entertained them, until a tall, lanky farm boy ambled out to the microphone and launched into his "Lovesick Blues." Hank Williams stopped the show. Minnie Pearl said, "everybody, me included, rushed to the wings of the stage," and Little Jimmy Dickens remembered that "there were so many encores that I lost count of 'em." Others say the number was six and that Red Foley had to calm the crowd by promising that Hank Williams would be heard again on the Opry.

Mr. Grant Turner, who joined the Opry as an announcer in 1944, said that he knew something momentous was happening that night: "The fans just didn't want to let him go. When Hank would work that stage, he would appear to be suspended in a blue haze, very much as if you had a coat hangar in his suit holding him up over the microphone. He just had that way of being totally relaxed, and, he being a Southerner and knowing his audiences so well, had that easy-going drawl in his voice and manner that made people love him so much." Mr. Turner also described Williams in moments of repose: "Hank had a way of sitting on a couch, all slumped down, and he would wind one foot around the other. He would cross his leg and hook that toe back around the other leg—all wound up like a corkscrew." Mr. Turner likened Hank Williams' stage appeal to that of another

Mrs. Naff meets with the Auditorium Improvement Board in 1948 to inspect renovations to the Ryman. Special Collections/ Vanderbilt University Library

Opry legend, Uncle Dave Macon.

The early fifties saw other bright additions to the Opry's growing constellation of stars: Hank Snow in 1950 and Martha Carson and Faron Young in 1952. The Carter Family, Mother Maybelle, Helen, June and Anita, joined the Opry in 1951. Chet Atkins was their guitarist, and many a fan felt much as Dottie West remembered feeling when she heard them in the Ryman:

"We all know it was built as a tabernacle, and I would cry sometimes when I heard Anita's pure, sweet voice in that old building. It was just like hearing an angel sing."

An angel of a different type also shared the stage with the Carter Family. Kitty Wells brought her number one hit, "It Wasn't God Who Made Honky Tonk Angels," to the Ryman in 1952, and paved the way for other women to join the Opry. Just as Roy Acuff is country music's king, Kitty Wells remains its queen.

Hank Williams left the Opry in 1952, and Webb Pierce arrived. So did Jumpin' Bill Carlisle who remembered that he was "real nervous" to be playing in the Ryman Auditorium. Among his early memories of the Ryman was "seeing all those

Opry announcer Grant Turner, June Carter, and Archie Campbell "cut a rug" on stage at the Ryman. Grand Ole Opry Archives

hand fans in the summertime. Old-timey hand fans." Laughingly, he poked gentle fun at the present-day Opry management: "That's one thing they should of thought about before they moved us out of the Ryman. They lost their sales on all them hand fans when they moved out to an air-conditioned building."

Del Wood, Marty Robbins, Jim Reeves, the Louvin Brothers, Jean Shepard, and Justin Tubb all joined the Opry roster in the early fifties. In 1954 a non-member made his only appearance: Elvis Presley. Although some have said he never did perform at the Ryman, among those who emphatically do remember that one appearance are Justin Tubb, who took the young singer to his father's record shop afterwards, and Little Jimmy Dickens, who said: "I certainly do remember his one and only performance on the Grand Ole Opry. I was very interested in Elvis. I had been hearing his records and "Blue Moon of Kentucky" was catching on, the old Bill Monroe song with the Elvis touch. His record was just getting real good and hot, and I'd been looking forward to hearing this young man. He came to the Ryman, and I was so anxious to see how the audience of the

Opry favorite and country music legend Hank Williams per-
forms at the Ryman with Chet Atkins on guitar. Grand Ole Opry
Archives

Grand Ole Opry would respond. Really, the response was not that good. Elvis didn't click at all on his first and only appearance. Our audience was there for the dyed-in-the-wool country music, and that's not exactly what Elvis was doing."

The story goes that Jim Denny, the Opry's talent manager, told Elvis that he ought "to go back to driving a truck." Elvis cried all the way back to Memphis. Skeeter Davis remembered Elvis musing aloud to her, "I wonder why they don't like me at the Opry, because Marty Robbins gets up there and does my songs and they love him."

Aside from "rockabilly," the Ryman saw other innovations in the early fifties. By this time country and pop music had blended into a sound which made many songwriters and artists rich and famous. Recordings were even made in the Ryman itself. For example, whenever Castle Studios wanted to record Red Foley, with orchestral accompaniment, they did it from the Auditorium. In an article for the *Journal of Country Music* (December 1978), music historian John Rumble explains how: "On sessions taking place in the Ryman involving orchestra and/ or background vocalists, the engineers kept their cutting lathe at the Tulane Hotel. They fed the electrical impulses from microphones at the Ryman through a telephone line rented for this purpose." Probably the earliest date for a recording done in the Ryman was the one of April 9, 1952, found by Rumble in the Castle Studio logbooks.

Television also came to the Ryman in 1954 with a network program, sponsored by Ralston Purina, which aired the fourth week of every month. Of course, Minnie Pearl, Rod Brasfield, and Roy Acuff were featured on those early television shows. The ABC show, "Stars of the Grand Ole Opry," was filmed an hour or so before the Opry, which began at 7:30 p.m. In that way the producers used the Opry crowd as an audience for the filming. Minnie Pearl remarked that "Purina seemed pleased with it, since they got to sell a lot of bulk feed for hogs and cows. They'd set those sacks there on the stage, and Roy and I had to sit on them sometimes for publicity shots. One time, some real smart ad-man decided to do a fan mail poll, and they asked Roy and I to make the pitch. Roy told all the people who were watching to write a card or letter and just to tell us that they were watching, not whether they liked the show or not. Well, they got so many cards and letters that they had to hire ten

Anita Carter, Mother Maybelle Carter, Helen Carter, Ferlin Husky, Chet Atkins, Jean Shepard, Carl Smith, Minnie Pearl, the Collins Kids, Buddy Ebsen, June Carter, Earl Scruggs, Lester Flatt, and the Jordanaires appear on the Ralston Purina television show in 1955. Grand Ole Opry Archives

secretaries to handle them all. They divided them up into rural, urban and suburban stacks, and found out that they were from the urban and suburban viewers. Well, Purina was trying to sell feed to rural people, and so they cancelled the show."

Another early television show cited by present Opry Manager Hal Durham was a Christmas special for Martha White Flour, a loyal Opry sponsor that saw a dramatic growth in sales after it began advertising on the Grand Ole Opry. Through the next twenty years, television cameras became a routine fixture in the Ryman, with Arlene Francis, Dinah Shore, Barbara Mandrell, and Dolly Parton all shooting segments of their shows there, and Jimmy Dean and Porter Wagoner using the Auditorium for their weekly variety shows.

Johnny Cash insisted on having his show filmed in the Ryman. When he had first appeared on the Opry in 1956, he had been a sensation. Carl Smith introduced him as "the brightest rising star in country music of America," and Minnie Pearl told

63

Johnny Cash in an early appearance at the Ryman. Grand Ole Opry Archives

the adoring crowd, "If I was thirty years younger and thirty pounds lighter, we'd be courting tonight." When he finished singing "I Walk The Line," the No. 2 song in the nation at the time, the crowd stood and roared its approval. Cash never forgot the warm welcome of the audience or the help of the Opry regulars who had lobbied for his appearance that night. He also never forgot the hall itself, and years later, when he could call the shots, he demanded that ABC's "The Johnny Cash Show," which premiered June 7, 1969, be filmed in the Ryman. That show brought a new breed of entertainer to the Ryman, the rock star.

At the time Cash told a reporter for the *Tennessean*, "I love that old building. I love the feeling it gives me, and I love the people." Johnny Cash did not want a Hollywood studio or a Hollywood audience for his variety show; he wanted the real thing and knew that he would find it only in Nashville at the Opry House. His production staff, some thirty strong, moved to Nashville. An acoustical engineer from Texas advised them how best to adapt the Ryman for the program, and they converted an old tavern across the alley from the Auditorium's back door into a series of offices and dressing rooms.

For each taping they parked their trailer, jammed with studio equipment and technical material, at the back door, and they had scenery and props built in a nearby workroom and brought over to the Ryman. Before the programs could be taped, the staff had to build an extension onto the old Opry stage over which they laid special flooring. All of their labor lasted only as long as the taping, since the Ryman had to be restored to its everyday appearance before Friday nights. The whole process took over ten hours. Johnny Cash knew what others found out slowly but surely—that the Auditorium had become a part of the show.

Dee Kilpatrick took over from Jim Denny in 1956 as the Opry's general manager and as manager of WSM's Artist Services Bureau. He believed strongly that the Opry needed a mix of traditional entertainers and newer, younger stars to balance its appeal. To attract new fans, he brought in Ferlin Husky, Rusty and Doug Kershaw, and the Everly Brothers. Futhermore, he delighted the traditionalists by continuing the ban on drums ("symbols of rock and roll") at the Opry House, but antagonized them at the same time by consolidating four of the original string bands into two groups, the Crook Brothers, and the Fruit Jar Drinkers.

Of course the Opry brought other events to the Ryman in the early fifties. Annual Disc Jockey Conventions and later the Country Music Association Awards were held in the Ryman.

Lester Flatt and Earl Scruggs (at the microphone) perform at the Ryman Auditorium with (left to right) Lightning Chance, Paul Warren, Jake Tullich, and Josh Greene. In the right foreground, Opry announcer T. Tommy Cutrer contemplates his next remarks, and, in the left background, the ever-watchful Opry manager Vito Pellettieri makes sure things run smoothly.
Grand Ole Opry Archives

True to the spirit of the building, Wally Fowler held his inter-denominational All-Night Gospel Sings there. The first one occurred on November 4, 1948, and continued for several years on the first Friday of each month. At times the audience for Wally Fowler's "Sings" rivaled the Opry's own in numbers and enthusiasm.

In 1955, Lula C. Naff retired as manager of the Ryman, and her assistant of four years, Harry Draper, took over the job. Road shows like *Oklahoma* and *Back to Methusalah* continued to play the Ryman, as did theatrical stars like Carol Channing and Victor Borge. But the real business of the Ryman had become the Opry.

Jimmy C. Newman and Stonewall Jackson joined Johnny Cash in becoming its newest stars in 1956. Wilma Lee and Stoney Cooper, Ferlin Husky, and Porter Wagoner joined them in 1957, and a little girl from Sevierville, Tennessee, Dolly Parton, sang one song on the Friday Night Frolics. The Stoney

*Dolly Parton and Porter Wagoner sing one of the duets for
which they were beloved by their fans.* Grand Ole Opry Archives

Patsy Cline, an Opry favorite, performs at the Ryman Auditorium, where later her fellow performers would pay tribute to her and three others who died tragically in a plane crash in West Tennessee. Grand Ole Opry Archives

Mountain Cloggers brought their versions of mountain dances to the stage that same year. The last years of the fifties brought other new talent to the Ryman: Del Reeves, Skeeter Davis, Jan Howard, Archie Campbell, and George Hamilton IV.

But there were also painful times. Rod Brasfield died of a heart attack in 1958, and in 1959 the Opry's beloved stage manager, Vito Pellettieri, faced mandatory retirement. Every one of the Opry performers signed a petition asking WSM to allow him to remain, if not in his post as music librarian, at least as Opry stage manager. Often called "The Contrariest Man Alive," Mr. Pellettieri had for years turned the total confusion of Saturday nights on the Ryman stage into the "organized chaos" that was the Opry. WSM officials, overwhelmed by the entertainers' demands that he remain with the show, relented, and he continued to goad his "family" to give their best performances.

Hank Locklin and Bill Anderson both became regular performers in the early sixties, and on the distaff side Patsy Cline and Loretta Lynn began appearing regularly. One need not be an

Opry fan to realize the impact of these two women on the music industry. Certainly one of the saddest events in the Ryman's long history, a history which had seen memorial services for such men as Sam Jones, William McKinley, William Jennings Bryan, Governor Austin Peay, and Theodore Roosevelt, was the short interruption in the Opry on Saturday night, March 9, 1963, for a tribute to five of its entertainers who had died that week. Ott Devine, who was manager of the Grand Ole Opry, asked the audience to stand with the assembled performers that night for a silent prayer of tribute to Patsy Cline, Cowboy Copas, Hawkshaw Hawkins, Jack Anglin, and Randy Hughes. The Jordanaires then sang "How Great Thou Art," and the Opry resumed.

These were also important years in the history of the building itself. In 1961 the Ryman had celebrated its 70th birthday with a gala performance by the American Ballet Theater. For that evening the old Tabernacle came alive with gas lights on its sidewalks, antique cars at its doorstep, and a red carpet and canopy covering its stairs. At the same time some of the Opry's stars invaded Carnegie Hall for a rousing, sold-out performance. Despite their success, Dorothy Kilgallen, popular New York columnist, raised the ire of many an Opry-lover when she referred to the visitors as "hicks from the sticks."

The Ryman still hosted conventions, revivals, sporting events (wrestling matches, for example), fine arts programs, and even an occasional livestock show. One of the earliest events in the Union Gospel Tabernacle had been a performance by the celebrated horse, Jim Key, but these later shows in the Ryman featured purebred cattle exhibitions. Grant Turner explained how the cattle got onto the stage: "They brought them in the back door. There was one entrance to the Opry House that was probably used to bring in heavy equipment, and they could run those cattle down from the truck right through the door. Once inside the Opry House, they could lead them to the stage through a series of ramps. Those cattle could walk on those ramps with no problem at all right to the stage. They probably put a tarp over the stage and then straw over that to have their cattle show."

Because of competition and the scarcity of good shows, Mr. Draper was unable to give Nashville the same kind of music and theater that Mrs. Naff had gotten in the 1930s. Yet he too leapt to the defense of the Ryman as a home for the Opry when a letter in the *Tennessean* suggested that it was an inappropriate locale. In his rejoinder Mr. Draper maintained that "much of" the Opry's "fabulous appeal, which is international," would disappear in any other location. He believed that the Opry and the Ryman were perfectly compatible.

National Life got the opportunity to show that they shared his belief when they bought the Ryman from its Board on September 27, 1963, for $207,500. Negotiations for another long-term lease had fallen through, and the insurance company decided that, rather than pay $20,000 a year in rent, it made better sense to buy the building. National Life immediately renamed it the "Grand Ole Opry House."

WSM set about quickly to remodel the building and to make repairs, some necessitated by a ruling from Actors Equity that prohibited its union members from working shows there. Actors from a touring company of *Luther* had complained that cables stretched across the backstage area were a safety hazard and that the building was "unsanitary." WSM, which had just spent over $25,000 on improvements, negotiated a reversal of the order with Actors Equity. When fire marshals deemed the building structurally sound and in good repair, the union rescinded its ban.

The growing number of people who wanted to see the Friday Night Frolics finally forced WSM to move the weekly event to the Ryman in 1964. Again, Studio C had become too cramped. Roy Acuff explained, "They had to move it. I'd tell people to come see it, and they wouldn't be able to get in the studio. They'd blame me and so I was glad they moved it on over to the Ryman." In the transfer the "Frolics" became the "Friday Night Opry."

The fans forced another alteration to the schedule in 1966. The summer months saw such vast numbers of people who wanted tickets, that the Grand Ole Opry began Saturday matinee performances to accommodate its fans. On one July weekend 15,000 people had tried to get tickets for one of the shows, and the Opry had been forced to stage a late performance from 12:30 until 2 at night. By early July in 1966 all reserve tickets through September 1 had already been sold out.

In 1964 the Opry listed fifty-five star acts and a total cast of over 100 performers. New ones appeared annually: Marion

Worth, Ernie Ashworth, the Browns, Dottie West, Willie Nelson, and the Osborne Brothers in 1963. But in 1964 the Opry lost some of its biggest attractions. Jim Reeves died in a plane accident, and for failure to appear on the required 26 shows a year, the Opry dropped 11 stars from its roster: Kitty Wells, Ray Price, George Morgan, Don Gibson, Billy Grammer, Johnny Wright, the Jordanaires, Faron Young, Ferlin Husky, Justin Tubb, and Stonewall Jackson.

The last years of the sixties saw other artists added: Tex Ritter, Bobby Bare, Norma Jean, Bob Luman, Ray Pillow, Stu Phillips, Jack Greene, Charlie Walker, Jeannie Seely, the 4 Guys, and last but not least Dolly Parton.

Unfortunately, Johnny Cash and the Opry parted company for a few years in 1965. In his autobiography, *The Man In Black*, he described that night in the Ryman, a night when he began to realize that pills were taking a devastating toll on his life: "The band kicked off a song, and I tried to take the microphone off the stand. In my nervous frenzy I couldn't get it off. Such a minor complication in my mental state was enough to make me explode in a fit of anger. I took the mike stand, threw it down, then dragged it along the edge of the stage, popping 50 or 60 footlights. The broken glass shattered all over the stage and into the audience." Ott Devine, then Opry manager, quietly told Cash backstage that the Opry would no longer be able to use him.

NBC's telecast of the Second Annual CMA Awards in 1968 required many temporary changes in the Opry House. A whole new stage laid down over the old one projected eight or nine rows into the space vacated by the pews. The producers redecorated the stage to mask its more rustic aspects and hung white, starry lights throughout the area. The awards show was a success, and until the Opry moved out it was an annual event in the Ryman.

In the early seventies the Opry added performers who had the good fortune to spend part of their careers in a building that had become synonymous with country music. The group included Tom T. Hall, David Houston, Barbara Mandrell, Connie Smith, Jerry Clower, and Jeanne Pruett, who proudly pointed out that she was "the last singing artist to join the Grand Ole Opry while it was still at the Ryman Auditorium." Sadly, beloved Dave "Stringbean" Akeman was killed in a grisly assault in 1973, the year before the move into the new Opry House.

Aside from its regular Opry broadcasts from the Ryman, WSM hosted other events from the Auditorium: the annual Opry Birthday Celebration and country Disc Jockey's Convention (since 1951), the Fan Fair (since 1971, in concert with the Country Music Association), and Grand Ole Gospel Time (a Sunday afternoon show created by E. W. Wendell to recognize the close links between country and gospel). Jimmy Snow, Hank Snow's son, also hosted a gospel show which followed the Friday Night Opry in the Ryman. In addition, the Auditorium was the scene for beauty contests, talent shows, and marriages. Brother Oswald was married at the Ryman, and he and Roy Acuff occasionally served as "best men" for couples who wanted a lifetime memory of being married in the Opry House.

IV. Mother Church: Nights at the Opry

For those who never experienced the Grand Ole Opry in the Ryman Auditorium, fortunately we have the testimony of its stars, its fans, and its historians. Though many became so emotional in the retelling that they groped for words, the experiences they described vividly bring back to life the Ryman's history.

From these stories, one can imagine, for example, scores of people standing under the hot, summer sun, four to eight abreast and forming lines stretching for blocks on some days. All were waiting for tickets to the Opry, and some of them, over 9,000 for one night in 1955, would wait three to four hours to get into the Ryman.

Porter Wagoner never forgot the sight: "I came in from the road one Saturday morning and got off the bus and started home. I drove up Broad Street and saw people lined up six abreast all the way from the Ryman around the corner of Broad. For a whole block down Broad! Just waiting to get tickets to see the Grand Ole Opry. This was at 6:30 a.m. I remembered that I'd waited in line, too, when I was 14 years old. How important country music could be to these fans that they would wait for five hours just to get tickets! I can't express how I felt when I saw that happen."

Souvenir sellers hawked their wares to the crowd. Ushers kept fans in line with ropes and bullhorns, and evangelical preachers (fittingly given the Ryman's roots in religion) shouted at them and passed out tracts. The fans, dressed in everything

Long lines stretching down the street were a familiar sight during the fifties as fans flocked to see the Grand Ole Opry.
Opryland USA Inc photo

from overalls and brogans to Sunday clothes, stood patiently, expectantly. Grant Turner often saw a man selling "rooster whistles," and on Saturday afternoons downtown Nashville sometimes sounded like a chicken coop when small boys tried out this ingenious toy. Occasionally winos asked people in line for some spare change, then shuffled away.

Ticket in hand, the anxious fan rushed to his seat on the hard, timeworn pew. One patron remarked, "This is a nice place to visit, but I sure wouldn't want to sit here." "Punishment, pure and simple, to get your butt scalded raw," was how Roy Acuff gruffly described it. You could always buy a souvenir cushion, if it got unbearable. You could even buy two seats for yourself, if you had to, as one extremely obese, loudly-dressed lady evangelist did.

Minnie Pearl hungrily recalled the box lunches the fans brought, baked ham and fried chicken and potato salad, which they washed down with soft drinks from the Ryman's concession stands. Infants in arms got their meals too, since it was not unusual to see mothers nursing their children during performances.

By this time in the evening parking was nonexistent around the Ryman. Every manner of conveyance, Cadillacs and buses for the stars, Fords and Chevys for the fans, fought for space throughout the neighborhood. Grant Turner described how enterprising truck owners in small towns loaded up their flat beds with people and drove into Nashville on Saturdays. The ride back in the forties probably cost about the same as a ticket to the Opry.

Heartbroken fans who couldn't get in stood on the outside and looked through the windows that ticketholders, desperate for a little cool air, had flung open. So hot was the Ryman in July that Roy Acuff said, "It made my head swim to see all those hand fans a-pumpin' out there. I'd get so dizzy I'd have to close my eyes."

On the stage the Opry-lovers saw dancers, singers, comics, announcers, and stagehands in a frenzy of activity, because after all, this was a radio show and had to keep to a fairly rigid timetable. When asked if it seemed like organized chaos, Jeannie Seely retorted, "More like 'accidental organization,' if you ask me." Backdrops advertising Martha White Flour, R.C. Cola, Jefferson Island Salt, or Prince Albert flew up and down at

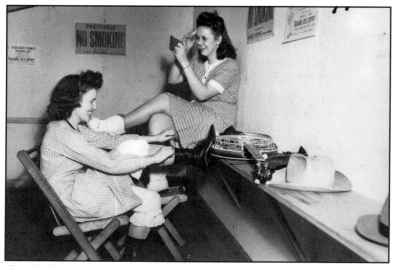

Rachel Veach and Velma Williams prepare for their set with Roy Acuff's band. Grand Ole Opry Archives

the appointed time. Different colored footlights illuminated a quick set change to a farmhouse. June Carter liked to sit in a rocking chair to enjoy the rest of the show when she wasn't performing. Ben Smathers and the squaredancers took their hard-earned breaks on benches on the left side of the stage. People milled around, gossiping, laughing and "cutting up." Hank Snow got so hot sometimes that he'd twirl his hankerchief in front of his face for a little fresh air, and Porter Wagoner brought two suits, one was always sweat-drenched before he finished his first show.

Comics kept the crowds in stitches, especially in the forties and fifties. Roy Acuff's band generally had a routine where one member unravelled a shirt stuffed into his pants some twenty feet across the stage. Lonzo and Oscar mugged and gamboled, whether it was their spot or not.

The best seats probably were in the balcony, and lucky was the sideman who had his girlfriend in the section over the wings so that he could join her between sets. "Unlucky," according to Jerry Rivers, fiddler for Hank Williams' Drifting Cowboys, "was the star who had his wife and girlfriend up there at the same time."

The Crook Brothers rehearse for their spot on the Opry in one of the Ryman's cramped backstage rooms. Grand Ole Opry Archives

Backstage the Crook Brothers, the Gully Jumpers, and the Fruit Jar Drinkers got together for impromptu jams in one of the dressing rooms. The banjo player might have had to stand out in the hall to try out his new material. Sometimes, Jan Howard recalled, "it would get so crowded back there that you had to leave in plenty of time or you'd miss your spot." The men had primitive, cramped dressing rooms; the women had only a restroom.

The bathroom is still a sore point for some "country women." Barbara Mandrell described it for Chet Hagan: "You know what I recall most about the old Ryman? It's dressing and getting made-up and all in the toilet, which was the woman's dressing room. That was really close, and warm and friendly, sharing that crowded space with Loretta Lynn and Connie Smith and Dolly Parton and Jeannie Seely."

Many things happened in that ladies' room. Jan Howard had a run-in with Patsy Cline which ended in a warm friendship. An innocent Skeeter Davis learned some of the seamier secrets of show biz. Dottie West saw "girls sitting on the floor trying to get dressed, sitting on some other things trying to get dressed too. I'm not going to tell you where my spot was, but, anyway, it was always a mighty full room." When Too Slim of Riders in the Sky asked Jeannie Seely "with virtually no dressing area, how did they handle men and women backstage?," she laughed, "That's how all the older members of the Opry got to know each other." Backstage was no place for modesty.

When entertainers left the building, they found their fans waiting. If they were only going over to Tootsie's Orchid Lounge for a drink or Linebaugh's for something to eat, they stopped and chatted for a minute. Porter Wagoner and Dolly Parton ran into a logjam of fans one night as they made their way hurriedly to their bus. He recalled: "After our spot we had to leave immediately to head for a matinee show in Pennsylvania the next day. When we got out the back door, there was just fans everywhere, unbelievable. This was just after Dolly and I had won the CMA Award at the Ryman Auditorium [1968] for best duet of the year, and she and I were very popular with the fans. I would have loved to have stopped and signed autographs, but we couldn't do it and make our commitment to the show. So I told the people when we came out, 'Now wait a minute. We can't sign autographs, because we are in a rush.' I explained about the next day's show and said, 'It's not fair for us to sign one or two when there are so many of you, so I hope that y'all will understand and forgive us.' Well, one lady just kept after us; she followed us and kept on saying, 'Just sign mine, just sign my autograph book.' I told her, 'Lady I can't just sign yours. It wouldn't be right for me to sign yours and not sign anyone else's.' She pestered us all the way to the bus. When I opened the door and stepped inside, we heard her say, 'Well, I'm sure glad I voted for Conway and Loretta last year.'"

Local characters frequented the area around the Ryman. Jerry Rivers talked about one man nicknamed "City View" who lived in a cardboard shack on the roof of Tootsie's. Hal Durham remembered a man called "Up-the-Alley-O'Malley." Roy Acuff was known as an "easy mark" for the panhandlers, and Ernest Tubb even set up an account at one of the neighborhood restaurants for the winos. None of them ever used that account. Stars, fans, winos, even an occasional prostitute mingled and mixed at the Ryman's back door.

Something was always going on back there, according to Chet Atkins. Undiscovered songwriters, singers, and musicians begged for a chance to display their talents. Sometimes, as Jerry

Rivers revealed, someone would oblige: "George Morgan and Robert Lunn (Roy Acuff's "Talking Blues Boy") used to audition people out in the alley. There was an old outhouse out there with a corrugated tin roof, and people would be standing around in front of it. Some old boy would ask Mr. Acuff, 'Roy, please just give me a chance to show you what I can do,' and he'd tell 'em, 'Well, son, you're just going to have to talk with Mr. Lunn. He's the boss around here.' Then somebody would go tell Robert that he had an appointment out in the alley. He would come on out and ask the boy, 'Well, what can you do?'

'I'm a singer.' They were always singers.

'Can you dance?' Robert Lunn would ask. 'We got plenty of singers, but we're always looking for somebody on the Opry that can dance.'

'Well, yeah, I can learn to dance.' And the first thing you know, they can dance, and they'd just whip into it. But Robert always told them, 'I can't tell anything by that, you've got to be like you're on a stage.'

In a minute, the tin roof on that old shanty would just be a'rattlin'."

The shenanigans did not stop at the back door. George Morgan was infamous for his practical jokes. In the days when Jerry Rivers played for Bill Monroe, Carl and Pearl Butler, and Cowboy Copas, he recalled that there just weren't that many good slide guitar players around, "aside from Don Helms who was one of the very best." One of the novice players was in such a learning stage that he had a piece of masking tape on the neck of his guitar with the notes written on it. "So, Shot Jackson went out and peeled that tape up and moved it a fret. And it worked out that the old boy played a fret sharp all night. He'd hear that it wasn't right, and he'd look down at the tape and it would still be in the same place." The other sidemen tried hard to hide their laughter.

Every night at the Opry was a special night, but for those fans who had driven miles and miles just to hear and to see Marty Robbins, there were special treats in store. Robbins in his later career developed a strong bond with his fans. One woman even tried to disrobe for him at the Ryman one night right in front of the stage, but Marty calmed her down. He liked to race cars on Saturdays and therefore preferred the latest time slot, 11:30 p.m., on the schedule. He usually kept going well after

Marty Robbins made his first appearance at the Ryman in 1953 and was soon invited to join the Opry. Grand Ole Opry Archives

midnight when the other entertainers had already left for home or gone over to the Ernest Tubb Record Store for the Midnight Jamboree. After he finished playing and singing, he would sit on the edge of the stage and talk and visit with his fans. When the ushers finally had to close the Ryman, he would sometimes go out on the front steps and sign autographs until the wee hours of the morning. Hal Durham said, "He had to tip the street cleaner who couldn't get his work done for all the people waiting for a chance to talk with Marty."

The Opry regulars have their own vivid memories of performances by their friends and colleagues in the Ryman Auditorium. Dolly Parton maintains that she didn't know the meaning of the expressions "sex appeal" and "charisma" until she saw Johnny Cash on that stage. Porter Wagoner said that when he first went to the Ryman, Roy Acuff "had probably one of the best shows I'd ever seen in my life." Jeannie Seely remembered that the Osborne Brothers "just stopped me in my tracks" one night when they did 'Kentucky.' I had only heard it on the radio and when I heard it in that auditorium, and they did the part where the music stops and they just do the harmony part, I

Dottie West, Sonny Osborne, and Bobby Osborne (left to right) are pictured with Opry manager Ott Devine on the night of their induction into the Opry cast—August 8, 1964. Ironically, West died as a result of injuries she suffered in a 1991 car accident on her way to the Opry. Grand Ole Opry Archives

could hear them breathe. I thought to myself, 'The Osborne Brothers even breathe in harmony!'"

Dottie West made it a point to go up in the balcony to watch Marty Robbins. She described other special performances by Hank Williams, Mother Maybelle Carter, and Kitty Wells. Skeeter Davis looked forward to every performance by Loretta Lynn in the Ryman, because "she just seems to epitomize the best kind of country singer." Bill Carlisle was there for Patsy Cline's and Jim Reeves' first nights, performances which impressed him, but he always associates Stringbean with the old Opry House.

Jan Howard, of course, recalled the legends—Bill Monroe, Minnie Pearl, Roy Acuff, and Ernest Tubb—when they appeared in the Ryman, but she also remembered fondly others who made the Opry happen: "Mr. Norris and Mr. Bell, the guards, and Vito, the 'Grand Ole Man of the Grand Ole Opry,' as I called him." Mr. Norman Van Dame, presently a guard at the new Opry House and formerly one at the Ryman, stayed late

Loretta Lynn accepts the Country Song Roundup *1967 Favorite Female Artist Award from Opry Announcer Grant Turner.* Grand Ole Opry Archives

one night to watch Stonewall Jackson record from the stage of the old Tabernacle. Hank Williams "wasn't one of my favorites," he added, "but I'll tell you what. It was a dream to hear Patsy Cline singing in that old building."

Grant Turner had an abundance of special memories: Brother Oswald playing the dobro; Hank Snow and Porter Wagoner in their glittering Nudie suits; the sad, sweet songs, like "Molly Darling" by the Old Hickory Singers; Judge Hay blowing his whistle, Hushpuckenna; June Carter and Johnny Cash showing up unexpectedly; Uncle Dave Macon twirling his banjo; Patsy Cline in a wheelchair after her automobile accident; DeFord Bailey making guest appearances; and even a wide-mouthed Joe E. Brown appearing in *Harvey.*

For all these people the Ryman was a place of magic and mystery, of tradition and spirituality, of warmth and hospitality. Roy Acuff, who was fearful that some accident would befall the audience, said that the Ryman was a "wonderful old place," but one which had served its purpose perhaps too long. The family that is the Opry had outgrown the building, and they had to move on.

82

Friday night, March 15, 1974, was one of sorrowful anticipation for the Grand Ole Opry family. The next day they would be moving out of the Ryman Auditorium to a new home at Opryland USA. It was to be a special occasion, with such stars as Porter Wagoner and Dolly Parton flying in just for the two nights. Most paid tribute to the Ryman that Friday night with their songs, their words, and even with their tears. Minnie Pearl stood there, eyes streaming, and said, "It's going to be all right." The last thirty minutes of the program that night featured George Morgan, the 4 Guys, Ray Pillow, Lonzo and Oscar, and Ernie Ashworth. When the last song had been sung and the radio announcer had signed off, the Grand Ole Opry's tenure at the Ryman Auditorium was over.

But, the night was not yet over. Johnny Cash and June Carter, who share a fierce devotion to the Ryman Auditorium and its ghostly inhabitants, hosted one final gospel sing. The old hymns rose in praise of their and Sam Jones' and Captain Ryman's God. And appropriately, oh so fittingly, in that rounded, shabby interior, Johnny Cash led those assembled in one last prayerful song in the Ryman Auditorium, "Will the Circle Be Unbroken?" And then, just as Captain Ryman would have wanted it, one final word—Amen.

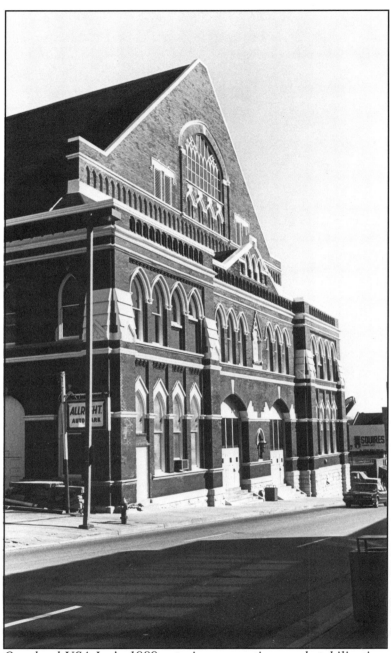

Opryland USA Inc's 1989 exterior renovations and stabilization project included the restoration of the Ryman Auditorium's 144 windows to glass. Donnie Beauchamp

84

Epilogue

In 1972 the Opryland theme park opened on a spacious tract east of Nashville proper, and, when the Grand Ole Opry moved to its new building there in 1974, the question of what to do about the Ryman was hotly debated by the public. The original plans called for the Auditorium to be razed, and its bricks used to erect a chapel at Opryland. Again Nashvillians, who, since its construction in 1892, had thought of the Ryman as theirs, let their voices be heard in opposition to this proposal. Genuinely surprised by the indignation and anger they had aroused, the planners decided to leave the Ryman where it stood. Its glory perhaps a little faded, it was yet part and parcel of the city's identity.

Today, a prime tourist attraction in Tennessee, the shrine that is the Ryman Auditorium attracts upwards of 200,000 visitors. It is a trek for many of them purposefully made, to rekindle memories of joyful nights in the old building, to see exactly where American musical history was made, or simply to "set and rest a spell" with the ghosts of yesteryear, as one devoted visitor acknowledged. "They're here, you know," she continued, "all the spirits of those opera stars and actors and preachers and singers. That's why I love this place. It's a warehouse of memories."

The old building still attracts stars along with the tourists. Movie fans have become acquainted with the "hallowed ground" that is the Ryman through such films as *W. W. and the Dixie Dancekings* and *Honky Tonk Man*. One movie, *Nashville*, considered by some critics to be one of the greatest accomplish-

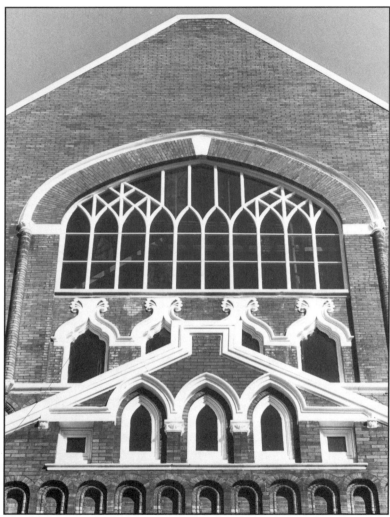

Architects studied old post cards, sketches, picture history books, and glass fragments to restore the Ryman Auditorium's arched pediment window which had been boarded up for some twenty years. Donnie Beauchamp

During the taping of her ABC variety show in 1988, Dolly Parton reminisced at the Ryman with (left to right) Del Wood, Jan Howard, Skeeter Davis, Minnie Pearl, Jeanne Pruett, Norma Jean, and Jean Shepard. Kitty Wells (not shown) also was present. Donnie Beauchamp

ments in world cinema, used the Ryman as a location for its climactic scenes. Robert Altman, the movie's distinguished director, saw the value of the interdenominational tabernacle as a metaphor not only for the city of Nashville but also for the country as a whole. More recently, Sissy Spacek starred in the inspirational story of Loretta Lynn in *Coal Miner's Daughter*, and Jessica Lange recreated Patsy Cline's poignant, tempestuous life in *Sweet Dreams*. What better location for the triumphs of these two women's lives than the Ryman Auditorium?

Other entertainers came as well. Dolly Parton returned to tape a part of a special for her variety show there in 1988. She invited "country women" to sit with her on that well-worn stage and reminisce about nights and afternoons under its spotlights. Emmylou Harris enhanced her reputation as a southern songbird when she taped a television special and a live album in the Ryman in 1992. In making plans for the concert, the only place suitable, the only place she had in mind as "special enough," was the Ryman. Plans call for its use in the future as a concert venue when only such a "special place" will serve.

The old Tabernacle, which underwent extensive exterior renovations in preparation for its centenary in 1992, may again serve as a symbol for all of Nashville. Plans are under way for it to become the focal point of a stabilization project for the downtown area immediately surrounding it. It also will continue to serve as an archive for the Opry, as a living museum of memories.

As one wise lady interested in historic preservation explained, "That old red brick building is the solid heart of Nashville." Truly, its mother church.

Selected Sources and Bibliography

Adams, George Rollie and Christian, Ralph Jerry. Nashville, A Pictorial History. (rev. ed.) Virginia Beach, 1988.

Axthelm, Pete. "A Tribute to the Ryman from the Bar at Tootsie's." *Newsweek*. March 25, 1974, p. 69.

"Bettie M. Donelson Papers." Tennessee State Library and Archives (II-E-2-3, 309).

Betts, Ann. "The Best One Night Stand in the Country." Premiere. Spring/Summer, 1985, vol. 5, no. 3, pp. 10-15.

Brumbaugh, Thomas B., Strayhorn, Martha, and Gore, Gary G., eds., Architecture of Middle Tenness*ee, The Historic American Buildings Survey*. Nashville, Tennessee 1974, pp. 40-47.

Cash, Johnny. *The Man in Black*. Zondervan Publishing House: Grand Rapids, Michigan, 1975.

"Charles S. Mitchell Collection." Vanderbilt University Library Special Collections. Donated by Jesse Wills.

Coke, Fletch. *Captain Ryman at Home; His Family and Neighbors on Rutledge Hill.* Nashville, Tennessee, 1982.

Cunniff, Albert. "Muscle Behind the Music: The Life and Times of Jim Denny." *Journal of Country Music.* Vol. XI, no. 1, 1986: "Part I, The Path to Power."

Custer, Jack E. "Captain Tom Ryman: The Man, the Myth, the Paradox." *Waterways Journal.* Jan. 27, 1979, pp. 11-81.

_____. "Capt. Ryman Revisited (or) Filling in the Gaps." *Waterways Journal.* Feb. 8, 1980, pp. 5-31.

Danker, Frederick E. "Country Music and the Mass Media: The Johnny Cash Television Show." *Popular Music and Society.* Vol. II, Winter 1973, no. 2, pp. 124-44.

"Darden Family Papers." Tennessee State Library and Archives (V-B-5, Ac-657).

Davis, Louise. "Steamboatin' Tom Ryman and His Gift to Nashville." *Tennessean Magazine.* Jan. 27, 1974, pp. 4-9.

_____. "When Captain Tom 'Got Religion'." *Tennessean Magazine.* Feb. 3, 1974, pp. 12-16.

_____. "The Men Who Built the Ryman." *Tennessean Magazine.* March 10, 1974, pp. 8-13.

Davidson, Bill. "Thar's Gold in Them Thar Hillbilly Tunes." *Colliers.* July 28, 1954, pp. 34ff.

Doyle, Don H. *Nashville in the New South, 1880-1930.* Knoxville, Tennessee, 1985.

_____. *Nashville Since the 1920s.* Knoxville, Tennessee, 1985.

Flamming, James Douglas. "The Sam Jones Revivals and
Social Reform in Nashville, Tennessee, 1885-1900."
(M. A. Thesis, Vanderbilt University) Nashville,
Tennessee, 1983.

"Francis Robinson Collection of Theater, Music, and Dance."
Vanderbilt University Library Special Collections.

Graham, Eleanor, ed. *Nashville, A Short History and Selected
Buildings.* Hist. Comm. of Metro-Nashville-Davidson
Co., 1974.

"Grand Ole Opry Collection." Vanderbilt University Library
Special Collections.

Hagan, Chet. *Grand Ole Opry.* New York, 1989.

_____. *Country Music Legends in the Hall of Fame.*
Nashville, Tennessee, 1982.

Hemphill, Paul. *The Nashville Sound: Bright Lights and
Country Music.* New York, 1970.

Henderson, Jerry. "A History of the Ryman Auditorium in
Nashville, Tennessee, 1892-1920." (Ph. D.
Diss., Louisiana State University) Baton Rouge,
Louisiana, 1962.

_____. "Nashville's Ryman Auditorium." *Tennessee
Historical Quarterly.* XXVII, Winter, 1968, pp. 302-28.

_____. "The Ryman Auditorium, Its Years as a Religious
Center of Nashville and the South." (unpub. paper)
Tennessee State Library and Archives, W-E-1, Box 1,
f. 9.

Holcomb, Walt. *Sam Jones, An Ambassador of the Almighty.*
Nashville, Tennessee, 1947.

Hope, Bob. "It Says Here." King Features Syndicate Press
Release. Jan. 27, 1949.

Incorporation Documents. *Official Records Book of Davidson County.* Copies made available with corporate books, letters and files of the Auditorium Improvement Company in possession of Mr. Roy A. Miles, Jr., Nashville, Tennessee.

Jones, Laura McElwain. *The Life and Sayings of Sam P. Jones.* Atlanta, Georgia, 1907.

Jones, Sam P. *Thunderbolts. Comprising Most Elegant Reasonings, Delightful Narratives, Poetic and Pathetic Incidents, Caustic and Unmerciful Flagellation of Sin, Together with Irresistible Appeal to the Higher Sensibilities of Man to Quit His Meanness and Do Right.* Nashville, Tennessee, 1896.

"Jeter Smith Dance Collection." Nashville Room, Nashville-Davidson County Public Library.

Keillor, Garrison. "Onward and Upward with the Arts at the Opry." *New Yorker.* May 6, 1974, pp. 46-48.

Malone, Bill C. *Country Music USA.* Austin, Texas, 1968.

McLoughlin, Jr., William G. *Modern Revivalism, Charles Grandison Finney to Billy Graham.* New York, 1959.

Miles, Jr., Roy A. "Obituary for a Grand Lady—The Ryman Auditorium." speech, Vanderbilt University, May 7, 1973.

Moore, Thurston, ed. *Country Music Who's Who.* Nashville, 1966. See esp. p. 28 for Stone, Harry. "Looking Back."

Nashville Banner. (Dates indicated in text.)

Nashville *Daily American.* (Dates indicated in text.)

Nashville Good News Weekly. (Dates indicated in text.)

Nashville *Tennessean.* (Dates indicated in text.)

Nashville This Week. (Dates indicated in text.)

Opry Picture/History Book. The Opry Observer. Nashville's Grand Ole Opry (text by Jack Hurst). All published in several eds. by the Grand Ole Opry, Nashville, Tennessee.

Pemberton, Brock. "The Theatre's 'Road' Staging a Comeback, but it is a Much Changed Road," *New York Times Magazine.* Aug. 20, 1939, copy s.p.

Pope, Bill. "Fiery Sam Jones Rose to Leading Evangelist." *Atlanta Constitution.* Nov. 21, 1961, p. 6.

Pugh, Ronnie. "Ernest Tubb's Performing Career: Broadcast, Stage and Screen." *Journal of Country Music.* vol. VII, no. 3, Dec. 1978, pp. 67-83.

Rensi, Raymond Charles. "Sam Jones: Southern Evangelist." (Ph. D. Diss., University of Georgia) Athens, Georgia, 1971.

Rivers, Jerry. *Hank Williams, From Life to Legend.* 2nd ed. Nashville, n.d.

Rumble, John. "The Emergence of Nashville as a Recording Center; Logbooks from the Castle Studio, 1952-53." *Journal of Country Music.* vol. VII, no. 3, Dec., 1978, pp. 22-41.

"Ryman Family Papers, 1841-1973." Tennessee State Library and Archives (V-L-5, Ac 81-15).

"Sam P. Jones Papers." Special Collections, Robert W. Woodruff Library, Emory University, Atlanta, Georgia.

"Sam P. Jones Papers." Hargrett Rare Book and Manuscript Library, University of Georgia Libraries, Athens, Georgia.

Schlappi, Elizabeth. *Roy Acuff, The Smoky Mountain Boy.* Gretna, Louisiana, 1978.

Smith, John L., compiler. *The Johnny Cash Discography.* Westport, Connecticut., 1985.

"The Naff Collection." Nashville Room, Nashville-Davidson County Public Library.

The Nashville Review. (Dates indicated in text.)

Thomas, Sr., Jack. *The Nashville I Knew.* Nashville, 1984.

"Wilhelmina Webb Collection." Metropolitan Nashville-Davidson County Archives.

Wilson, Richard L. "Sam Jones: An Apostle of the New South." *Georgia Historical Quarterly*, (57), 1983.

"WSM Radio/Television Collection." Vanderbilt University Library Special Collections. Donated by Jesse Wills.